Applying the
Blood

DESTINY IMAGE BOOKS BY DEREK PRINCE:

Applying the Blood

Blood

How to Release the
LIFE AND POWER OF
JESUS' SACRIFICE

Derek
PRINCE

DESTINY IMAGE® PUBLISHERS, INC.

P.O. Box 310, Shippensburg, PA 17257-0310

"Promoting Inspired Lives."

This book and all other Destiny Image and Destiny Image Fiction books are available at Christian bookstores and distributors worldwide.

Cover design by Eileen Rockwell

Interior design by Terry Clifton

For more information on foreign distributors, call 717-532-3040.

Reach us on the Internet: www.destinyimage.com.

ISBN 13 TP: 978-0-7684-5280-8

ISBN 13 eBook: 978-0-7684-5281-5

ISBN 13 HC: 978-0-7684-5283-9

ISBN 13 LP: 978-0-7684-5282-2

For Worldwide Distribution, Printed in the U.S.A.

1 2 3 4 5 6 7 8 / 24 23 22 21 20

CONTENTS

FOREWORD

MANY CHRISTIANS ARE FAMILIAR WITH THE WORDS OF "Power in the Blood," the old revival hymn: "There is power, power, wonder-working power in the precious blood of the Lamb." Every believer should be well aware of the profound spiritual truths embodied in those words. But are we?

In this book, *Applying the Blood*, we receive from Derek Prince a necessary foundation—not only a comprehensive exposition of the theological significance of the blood of Jesus, but also a helpful instruction manual regarding its practical application in our lives.

1

Derek Prince has approached this topic—first and foremost—with a profound sense of wonder and honor. Why is that so necessary and appropriate?

It is important because, as Derek comments in the book, solid biblical teaching on this subject is not always easy to find throughout the Body of Christ. We hear frequent references to the blood of Jesus in the normal course of conversations among Christians. But how many of us really understand its full impact or practical outworking in our life and faith?

Another significant reason to study this topic is the fact that many Christian traditions repeatedly use phrases like "pleading the blood" or "putting it under the blood" or being "covered in the blood of Jesus," sometimes to a degree that almost makes the phrase seem mundane or commonplace. However, as Derek readily points out, the lifeblood which was poured out by our Savior was anything but common.

The sacrifice of Jesus Christ, the Messiah—and the power released by the shedding of His blood in His passion—was and is extraordinary and phenomenal. Even more so when we put its power to work in our lives by using the biblical practices presented in this book. As this teaching unfolds, we trust that you, too, will be filled with a sense of honor, awe, and wonder at the profound significance of His outpouring for you.

Derek recognized that any focus on "blood" or any reference to "applying the blood" may cause a level of discomfort. In one section of *Applying the Blood*, he said: "There is always something a little bit disgusting about blood. I was a medical orderly in World War II, so I saw plenty of blood. But I also remember as a young boy, when I was about seven or eight years old, that if I saw blood...it had a real impact upon me emotionally. Even though I have grown past that kind of reaction, there is still something about blood that is very, very serious. Blood is a matter of life and death."

We can appreciate that kind of candid recognition on Derek's part. Even so, he followed these comments by asking you and me to persevere beyond any potential aversion to the topic. Here is Derek's goal for us—the result he hopes you and I will experience as we engage in our encounter with *Applying the Blood*: "I believe that if you will follow me through this teaching, it will give you a new insight into the life that is available to you and me thorough Jesus and the precious blood He shed on our behalf."

The International Publishing Team of
Derek Prince Ministries

Chapter 1

THE LIFE-TAKER AND
THE LIFE-GIVER

I WANT TO INTRODUCE THE TOPIC OF THIS BOOK,
Applying the Blood, by focusing on Jesus as the Life-
Giver—the One who gives life. The Bible, especially in
John's Gospel, clearly depicts two opposite persons. One
is the life-taker and the other is the Life-Giver. You and
I need to be able to identify both—to know how to resist
the workings of the life-taker and instead receive the
presence and power of the Life-Giver in our lives.

Let's begin our study of this concept by examining the
words that Jesus spoke in John 10:10:

The thief does not come except to steal, and to kill, and to destroy. I have come that they may have life, and that they may have it more abundantly.

This verse clearly reveals two opposing persons at work in the world—the thief who only comes to steal, to kill, and to destroy; and Jesus, who comes to give life and to give it more abundantly.

THE LIFE-TAKER

Who is the thief? You probably have little doubt about his identity. He is a person about whom Jesus regularly spoke and taught—an intensely evil being known as the devil or Satan. He is the *life-taker*. It is important for us to recognize that the devil is a real person—not a religious fiction or tradition, but a real spiritual being.

The American evangelist Oral Roberts used to say, and I think it is well worth repeating, "There is no goodness in the devil, and there is no badness in God. God is altogether good, and the devil is altogether bad." Those terms are not synonymous. Each has a specific significance.

To Steal

The devil comes to *steal*—that is, he desires to take away that which has been given us from God. His intent is to take away every good thing God wants us to have. What are those good things? Our innocence, our integrity, our peace of mind, our health, and the happiness of our homes and our families. When the devil comes, he comes with the intention of stealing all those.

Are you someone from whom the enemy has stolen much? Perhaps as you ponder this question, you are realizing that you have no peace of mind and no sense of personal identity. In fact, you feel troubled or insecure. Maybe you have been through the agonies of some family breakup. Perhaps you have never known who to blame. I am telling you now that the one responsible for your loss is the devil—the thief.

To Kill

Satan not only comes to steal; he comes to *kill*. He is a murderer. He comes to destroy us physically. Many, many people die before their God-appointed time, murdered by the devil. Alcohol and drugs are two of the devil's ways of killing people before their time. Alcoholics and drug addicts will rarely live out their full life span. Another way the devil kills people is with nicotine. It is a well-established medical fact that people who smoke will live a shorter time than people who do not smoke. In addition, smokers are extremely prone to major killing diseases—heart attack, lung cancer, and other similar maladies.

You and I need to know we are dealing with a murderer. He murders people psychologically—by the torment of insanity, fear, resentment, bitterness, and unforgiveness. All those are killers. Almost inevitably, people who fall prey to these psychological assaults will not live out their full life span.

One of the great requirements for health is a sense of security and peace of mind. When you lose those qualities, you are on your way to losing your health, even if you haven't already lost it. These are simple facts. They are not religious facts, but scientific, medical facts. They are facts of experience. Unless we listen to the warning of Jesus, we won't understand the identity of the person behind these physical and psychological assaults. It is the life-taker.

To Destroy

Jesus says that Satan not only comes to steal and to kill, but also to *destroy*. In light of the use of that word in the New Testament, my personal belief is that the destruction spoken of here goes beyond the present life span. The Bible says in Matthew 10:28 that God has authority to destroy both soul and body in a place called Gehenna. It is a place of torment, a place of fire, a place of unending agony—and that is the ultimate purpose of Satan for every person into whose life he comes.

Satan's intention is not merely to destroy you physically, emotionally, and financially in this life. His intention is not merely to bring you to an untimely grave. His goal is to see that you are destroyed forever—banished from the presence of God to a place about which Jesus spoke more than any other person in the Bible. Jesus said in Matthew 10:28:

> *And do not fear those who kill the body but cannot kill the soul. But rather fear Him who is able to destroy both soul and body in hell.*

SATAN'S METHODS

Scripture tells us the devil comes as a thief. Normally speaking, a thief doesn't announce who he is or why he has come. He doesn't approach in broad daylight, knock on your front door, and when you answer the door, announce, "Well, I'm a thief. I've come to take everything you have." Any thief wouldn't have much success that way. Even more the devil certainly does *not* take that approach. He doesn't tell you who he is or why he has come.

Likewise, a thief usually comes in the darkness of night so that his victim is not even aware he has come. Many times, the victim of a thief, who comes at night, wakes up in the morning to find that his or her most precious treasures have been taken while they slept through it all. Spiritually, that happens to many people. They don't even realize that the devil has taken precious treasures from them until they are gone. The thief came and went. They never saw him and never even knew who he was.

Another way thieves operate is by *deception*. We call these thieves confidence tricksters or con men. They come to their victims with fabricated stories, for instance, that they have discovered a new gold mine. Nobody knows about it yet, but they say it is going to produce unheard-of quantities of gold. They offer their victims an opportunity to purchase shares before the real value is known. "If you purchase shares now for ten pounds a share, in a few months, those shares will be worth a thousand pounds each."

In such a case, the victim may fall for the story and grab the opportunity to invest in this gold mine. But when that person has paid for and received the share certificates, they then discover that the shares are not worth the paper they are printed on. What's more, the thief is gone and so is all the victim's money.

The devil operates like that. He comes into your life and says he is going to give you a wonderful time—you are really going to enjoy yourself. You are going to have plenty of pleasure, plenty of money, plenty of leisure. But when you have bought into his deception, it isn't worth the price you end up paying.

There is another way thieves come. They come as robbers—armed men of violence. They burst in, confront you with a gun, and demand, "Where's your money? Where are your jewels? If you don't give them to us, we'll shoot you." They accomplish all of this by fear and pressure.

The devil operates that way in countless lives. I have heard so many people say, "I just couldn't take the pressure. It was too much for me. My mind snapped. I just had to give in. I couldn't hold out." Mental pressure, financial pressure, family pressure—and behind all those pressures is the enemy.

No matter what way the devil comes (and there are many other ways he could come), we need to write it on the tablets of our hearts: *he only has three motives—to steal, to kill, and to destroy.*

If you make him welcome, you are extremely foolish. Why? Because stealing, killing, and destroying is what he is going to do. We can't say, "I didn't know. I wasn't warned." Jesus warned us in the New Testament, and I am presenting His warning to you now: the thief only comes to steal, to kill, and to destroy. In fact, he has devastated too many lives already. He is the life-taker.

A CLEAR CHOICE

The good news, however, is that Jesus, the Life-Giver, came for the opposite purpose. He came not to take away, but to *give*. To give life—life more abundantly, spiritual life, physical life, a life that is exciting and full. To illustrate this, I would like to testify briefly to my own experience.

I was saved during World War II in the British Army in 1941. By profession, I was a professional philosopher. Before entering the army, I held a Fellowship in Philosophy in King's College in the University of Cambridge. When the war ended, the Provost of King's College wrote to me and made me a most attractive offer. If I would return to the College, he promised that in a few years I would be Tutor of the College. He promised that I would have a tremendous academic future in front of me.

Meanwhile, the Lord had called me to serve Him in Jerusalem. Faced with the choice between the two, I renounced my entire academic career. I gave it up. I entered into a life where my income was minimal and where I was confronted by many difficulties and pressures. For example, my first wife and I, along with our adopted family of eight girls, went through the tremendous turmoil and strife in the city of Jerusalem that marked the birth of the state of Israel. I would simply say that few people have experienced anything like what we experienced in Jerusalem. Twice we had to leave our home in the middle of the night to save our lives. We never knew who would be shooting at us or from what direction the shots would come.

Those difficult circumstances are what I accepted in exchange for a position at Cambridge University! But if I *had* accepted that position at Cambridge University, I would eventually have had to retire. Then I would simply be sitting in a little house somewhere with a moderate income, aging and burned out. Instead, here I am (five years past retirement age at the time of this teaching), strong and active. Indeed, I have had one of the most interesting, exciting, and challenging lives that anyone could imagine.

AN EXCITING LIFE

My first wife went to be with the Lord in 1975. When I married Ruth in 1978, I told her: "I think I can promise you one thing: our life will not be dull." I kept that promise; she would never have disputed that. Our life together was not always easy, but it was always rich and full. It has been exciting. I have had the inestimable privilege of giving myself to matters of eternal value—not just causes that have a certain amount of significance for a short period of time. I have invested in human lives in a way that will go on for eternity. I have imparted the truth of God—which lives forever and has the power to transform the lives of men and women. I have had the privilege to call people out of their darkness into the glorious light of Jesus Christ.

When I made that decision to leave my academic career, it seemed to be a sacrifice. But I will tell you, if I had to make the choice again, I would make the same decision. I have met a great many people who were called to serve the Lord and who responded to His call. When talking with them years later, I never met one who was dissatisfied with that decision. On the other hand, occasionally I met people who heard the Lord's call but refused. They thought at the time that the sacrifice was too great. Unfortunately, most of those people were somewhat bitter, discontented, and frustrated with their lives.

In the chapters that follow, I want to provide many insights into how Jesus loves us, how He gives us His *life*, and the great price that He paid. That price was the life-blood He poured out for us in His crucifixion and death. In the chapters ahead, we will discover how we can apply His very precious and powerful blood in a practical and effective way—a way that will change the course of our lives.

A MATTER OF LIFE AND DEATH

What I will share in this book is possibly a message that you have never heard. It centers in and focuses upon the blood of Jesus. In my opinion, far too little is preached in the contemporary church about the blood of Jesus. For the entirety of this book, I am going to dwell on that wonderful theme.

There is always something a little bit disgusting about blood. I was a medical orderly in World War II, so I saw plenty of blood. But I also remember as a young boy, when I was about seven or eight years old, that if I saw blood, I vomited. It had a real impact upon me emotionally. Even though I have grown past that kind of reaction, there is still something about blood that is very, very serious. Blood is a matter of life and death.

You and I might prefer to *not* face the facts about blood. But in this book, let's *choose* to face those facts. I believe that if you will follow me through this teaching, it will give you a new insight into the life that is available to you and me through Jesus and the precious blood He shed on our behalf.

Chapter 2

THE MEASURE OF GOD'S LOVE

IN THE FIRST CHAPTER, WE SAW HOW SATAN IS A *life-taker* who seeks to steal, kill, and destroy. In stark contrast to the life-taker, we saw the marvelous truth that Jesus came as a *Life-Giver*. He gave His life so that we could receive new life in Him. As we continue our study, let's reflect on how the Cross where Jesus poured out His life reveals the love of God. The cross shows the great price Jesus paid to redeem us.

If I had to choose one theme of the Bible as the greatest, I would have to say it is *the love of God*. Any study of the

Applying the Blood

death of Jesus on the cross that doesn't include some focus on the love of God is an incomplete study.

There are many possible ways of approaching the theme of God's love. But I am going to approach it by one particular route. The approach I will take is that we can discover the extent of God's love by the value that He set on us—and by the price that He paid for us. That is the way we will be looking at this subject. *What was the price that God was willing to pay for you and me?*

If you can receive this truth by faith, it will have a life-changing impact upon you. For example, it will do a great deal for your self-image. If you feel unimportant, unworthy, or in some way inferior, it is an indication that you have never understood the value God set upon you, which is the expression of His love for you. From the very beginning of this book, I believe it is important for us to recognize one basic truth: the love of God is so great that it really can't be measured.

WHY HE LOVES US

Actually, the love of God can also not be explained. Here is an interesting observation: nowhere in the Bible do you find an explanation of God's love. Let's begin with an interesting passage of Scripture in Deuteronomy 7,

18

where Moses is trying to tell Israel why God loved them. (These words apply to you and me as believers in Jesus.) In Deuteronomy 7:6, Moses says:

> *For you are a holy people to the Lord your God: the Lord your God has chosen you to be a people for Himself, a special treasure above all the peoples on the face of the earth.*

Do you realize that you and I are God's special treasure? After this initial statement, Moses attempts to tell Israel *why* God loved them. However, he never seems to reach a conclusion. Verse 7 says:

> *The Lord did not set His love on you nor choose you because you were more in number than any other people, for you were the least of all peoples.*

That statement is also true of you and me. We were the least. We were the foolish, the base, and the despised of the world. So why did God love us?

The next verse continues:

> *...but because the Lord loves you...*

God did not love you because you were this or that, but simply *because He loves you*. That seems to be the end of the explanation! You and I could search Scripture in vain for any explanation of God's love. The unexplained love of God is the ultimate fact behind history.

TWO PARABLES OF LOVE

Let's now examine some of the ways Scripture depicts the love of God. We will consider two parables found in Matthew 13. Right at the outset, let me state that the way I am interpreting these parables is by no means the only possible way. I know from the cross-references in the margin of my own Bible that whoever put them there interpreted the parables in a different way. It doesn't worry me, and you shouldn't let it worry you either. I would encourage you to consider what I am saying, because one of the features about parables is that they can be applied and interpreted in different ways in different contexts.

The two parables we are going to consider are the parables of the treasure in the field and the pearl of great price. They are both very short. The treasure in the field is just one verse. The pearl of great price is two verses. But the content is really *measureless*.

In Matthew 13:44-46, we read:

Again, the kingdom of heaven is like treasure hidden in a field, which a man found and hid; and for joy over it he goes and sells all that he has and buys that field.

Again, the kingdom of heaven is like a merchant seeking beautiful pearls, who, when he had found one pearl of great price, went and sold all that he had and bought it.

There is one feature common to each parable. The man in question found something so valuable that in order to obtain it, he had to part with everything else he had.

The Treasure in the Field

First, let us consider the picture of the treasure in the field. How did the treasure get hidden in the field in the first place? If you are familiar with the history of the Middle East, especially the land that was called Palestine, you will understand that it was frequently invaded by bands of marauders, all of whom came to plunder and steal.

We can picture a man with his house and all his valuables contained in it. News comes to him that marauders are on the way. He knows he can't hide his house. So, he takes a big wooden chest and piles all his valuables, money, and jewels into it. Everything that is of great worth goes into the chest. Then the man goes out at night, digs a hole in his field, and buries the chest. He covers it over, hoping that no one will find it. Perhaps in the ensuing fighting, he gets killed—and he was the only person who knew there was a treasure buried in that field.

The treasure may lie there for centuries. Who knows? Then, another man is walking across the field one day and he stubs his toe on a hard object. At first, he thinks it is a rock. But he looks down and sees a piece of wood. Wanting to find out what it is, he starts to dig it up. As he does, he finds a rotting old chest. As he pulls up just one corner of the lid, his eyes see jewelry, pearls, and gold. In that moment, he realizes what has happened.

The story in the Bible says that he hid the treasure again. Why? Because he didn't want anyone else to know there was treasure in that field. He wanted to keep that secret for one reason. What was it? The price of that field would have gone up significantly if anybody else found out about the treasure. Bear in mind this fact: The man didn't really want the field. He wanted the treasure. But in order to have a legal right to the treasure, he had to buy the field.

When he inquired about the price, it was a very high price. Some of the neighbors might have asked, "Whatever does that man want that field for? Nothing ever really grew in it. Why is he prepared to spend so much money on that field?" He doesn't tell anybody the real reason he wants it.

He knows the value of the treasure it holds, and he is very willing to pay the price.

The Pearl of Great Price

Let's now examine the other parable of the pearl of great price. It is very important for us to see that the man in this parable was a merchant. He was not a tourist. He isn't simply wandering through the streets of the town. He didn't simply happen upon some pearls in a shop window and listen to the story the owner told him about the merchandise. Instead, this man was looking intentionally. When he found this one pearl, he knew immediately it was unique. No other pearl he had ever seen equaled it. Not only was he a merchant, but he really loved his business. Once he had inquired as to the price of the pearl, he sold everything he had to pay for it. After he has bought the pearl, he holds it in his hand. He looks down at it and says, "I paid a lot for you. But you're worth everything I paid and more."

Now that you have heard both of these parables, I would like to interpret them for you. Please bear in mind that this is the "Prince" interpretation.

CLAIMING THE TREASURE

The man in both parables is a picture of *Jesus*. Really, in a sense He is the only one in a position to buy. Because you and I have nothing with which we can buy anything when it comes to the spiritual realm.

The *field* is interpreted by Matthew 13:38 where it says: *The field is the world*.

I believe this meaning runs consistently through the parables about the Kingdom of heaven in Matthew chapter 13. Every time *the field* is mentioned, it refers to *the world*. As Jesus looked at the world with His divine insight, He knew that hidden somewhere in the world was this priceless chest full of treasure. What was the chest, what was the treasure? Here is what I would like to suggest. The treasure is *God's people* whom He foreknew from eternity—the ones He chose for Himself.

Like the man in the story, in order to have legal right to the treasure, God had to buy the field. It wasn't really the field that He wanted. Rather, His interest was always the treasure in the field. What is the treasure in the field? It is God's people. People like you and me—and millions upon millions more. (In fact, there are a lot of those millions still in the field.)

Let's picture ourselves as the Lord's servants. God has paid the price for the field. What was the price? The precious blood of Jesus Christ. Our job now is to go out into the field and dig up the treasure. He has the legal right to it, but He gives us the privilege.

A lot of treasure remains under the earth to this day. It is all dirty and maybe it is corroded. A lot of work will need to go into getting the treasure out and making it what it ought to be. Please allow me to share a story that may increase your incentive to enter into the work that remains.

THE VIEW FROM THE TRAIN

Many years ago, in 1943, when I was a new Christian—I had only been saved two years—the British army sent me to the Sudan. This country is just south of Egypt, and at that time, it was administered by the British government. The word *Sudan* means "the black people." The people of Sudan were very primitive. The northern part of the

Sudan was totally Moslem, and the southern part was also very primitive and animistic, but becoming Christian. I worked for a short while in Sudan as a medical orderly. I had been put in charge of what they call the reception station at a railway junction in a town called Atbara in the northern part of Sudan.

I vividly remember my time traveling in the train as it went to Atbara from Khartoum. Because I was a British soldier, I had a carriage all to myself which none of the civilians could use. At one point in the train trip, we stopped at a platform in some city. If you have never been to a third-world country, you may not be able to picture this. But the platform was just totally alive with creatures of every kind: old men, old women, young men, young women, toddlers, babies being nursed by their mothers, donkeys, camels, chickens, dogs, etc. It was a seething mass of life.

As I looked out of the window at them from the carriage where I sat, I just said to myself, not in any kind of super-spiritual way: "I wonder what God thinks of these people." Surprisingly, I got an immediate answer from the Lord that has stayed with me to this day: "Some weak, some foolish, some proud, some wicked, and some exceedingly precious." As far as I am concerned, I have never had any reason to change that categorization of humanity: *some weak, some foolish, some proud, some wicked, and some exceedingly precious.* I believe that any time you and I look out over the mass of humanity there will be representatives of every one of those categories.

A DEEP CONCERN

When I arrived at Atbara, I was put in charge of the reception station—a place where soldiers were brought in if they were sick. In dealing with them, it would be my decision whether they needed medicine, whether they needed to go to the hospital, or whatever course of action might be required.

It is important for you to know at this point that the British Army never provided soldiers with pajamas. For my years in the army, I simply got used to sleeping in my underwear. However, at this reception station, there were not only two hospital beds, but also three white, flannel nightdresses. (The nightdresses were to be used by patients who required a bed.)

First of all, for me to have a really soft bed at that time was a luxury. As if that were not enough, I made another decision: "I'm going to sleep in a nightdress. I mean, here it is. Why shouldn't I use it?" So, I put this nightdress on and gloriously went to sleep in a nice, soft bed.

I don't know how to describe what happened next, but sometime during the night something supernatural occurred. In the middle of the night, I suddenly woke up with this tremendous burden to pray for the people of the Sudan. It was totally unexplainable. I have to say, in the natural no one would tend to find them very attractive people. But here I was, just pouring out my heart in prayer to God for these people whom I didn't know, and hadn't cared much about, outside of that holy moment.

Then, as I continued in my intercession, a miracle began to take place. My clothing became luminous. It was as if Jesus within me was shining through my body. I don't know if I can make this as clear as I would like, but Jesus began to speak to me about the way He loved those people. He spoke of them and others as His jewels. He reminded me that jewels are buried deep in the earth and that I had to mine them out. Then He said, "They are cut with suffering and washed with tears."

A FIRSTFRUIT OF HARVEST

After that short but meaningful stay in Sudan, I was deployed to a little place in the Red Sea Hills called Gebeit. Essentially, I spent the rest of the year in what was then called Palestine. I was put in charge of the "native" labor—pulled from area residents—in a very small hospital for Italian prisoners of war. Other than two doctors and a few people like me, the prisoners were the only people there. At that time, in 1943, there were thousands upon thousands of Italian prisoners of war under the care of the British Army. In this situation, I ended up being responsible to see that the native work force did its job.

The man in charge of the native labor force was a Sudanese named Ali, which is a very common Arabic name. To be blunt, he was a rogue. He cheated on the wages he got, kept back money given him, and he was a brawler. About the only positive word I could give to his credit was that Ali was a very good footballer (soccer player).

At first, Ali and I never seemed to be able to enter into any kind of relationship. Our routine was that I would meet him every morning, and we would talk together about what had to be done. He had learned English simply by talking to soldiers. He never had one lesson in English but had an amazingly accurate memory. For instance, one of the tasks we had to perform was the disinfestation of blankets. My British soldiers never could get the word *disinfestation* right, no matter how many times they tried. Ali heard that word once and never got it wrong after that.

For a while, we just didn't make any real connection. Then one day, I discovered that Ali believed in the devil. All Moslems do, though I knew nothing about Moslems at that time. I said: "I believe in the devil, too." Strangely enough, that became our point of contact. Every day, Ali would come to my little store (because I was also in charge of the rations for the hospital) and we would line up the day's work.

Over time, the Lord enabled me to bring Ali to faith in Jesus despite his Moslem background. This was a wonderful miracle, and the story of how it happened is an illustration of the point I am making about how precious people are. Ali was a clear example of what the Lord Jesus showed me that night in Atbara, before I ever got to Gebeit. On that train, He was showing a tiny little measure of His passionate love for even these not very loveable people.

Ali's tribe was called the Hadendoa. British soldiers called them "the Fuzzy-Wuzzies," because they habitually shaped their hair up about twelve inches above their head and greased it with mutton fat. We didn't find it very attractive, but the Lord loved them. Likewise, He imparted just a little bit of His love for them to me. During the time I was there in that hospital, Ali and one other workman got saved, and I baptized Ali in the hospital swimming pool before I left.

What the Lord showed me unmistakably through my relationship with Ali is that it is our responsibility as the Lord's servants to go into the fields and find the treasure. We have to unearth it, clean it up, remove the corrosion, the rust, whatever may be there, and make it fit to be presented to the Lord.

OUR TREMENDOUS VALUE

In the parable we examined earlier regarding the field, Jesus paid all that He had for that field. That is the measure of His love.

The parable of the pearl, as I said earlier, can be interpreted in various ways. I believe it is legitimate to interpret the pearl as *every redeemed soul*. It is important to understand that if there had only been one soul to be saved, Jesus (as the merchant seeking that pearl) would have paid the full price. This realization can really help you to have a sense of your own worth as a redeemed soul. *You* are the pearl of great price. Sometimes I imagine the joy experienced by that merchant when he bought that pearl. He didn't complain about the price. He was just satisfied he got the pearl.

Would you let your imagination run free for a moment? Would you allow yourself to picture that merchant with the pearl there in his hand? Imagine what he is saying as he talks to it: "Now you're mine. You belong to me. You cost me a lot, but I don't regret what I paid. You are the most beautiful pearl I have ever seen. You are altogether lovely. You are altogether perfect."

If you have any problems at all with self-worth, would you, just for a moment, picture yourself in the nail-pierced hand of the Lord Jesus. Imagine yourself saying, "I am that pearl. He died for me. He paid that price for me. If there had been no one else in all the world to be saved, He would still have paid the price for me."

NOT ONE BLEMISH

Among the books of the Bible, there are some very beautiful words in the Song of Solomon. If you can, allow your imagination to think of the words of the Song of Solomon as the Lord speaking to a redeemed soul. Or, you may want to interpret it as the Lord speaking to the Church.

But somehow, it is a little more exciting when you think about the Lord speaking to you personally. Listen to these words from Song of Solomon 1:15:

> *Behold, you are fair [or beautiful], my love!*
> *Behold, you are fair! You have dove's eyes.*

In Scripture, the dove is often a type of the Holy Spirit. Jesus is saying of you and me that we have eyes that see by the Holy Spirit. We can see Jesus as others can't.

Interestingly enough, I have been told—though I am not an expert on birds—that the dove is the only bird who has two eyes that can focus on a single object. Every other bird looks with one eye or the other eye. But the dove can focus with both eyes. When the Lord says to His beloved, "you have dove's eyes," it means you can see by the Holy Spirit. You can see Jesus as the single focus of your sight.

Then in Song of Solomon 4:7:

> *You are all fair, my love, and there is no spot in you.*

Isn't that beautiful? Not one spot, not one blemish. That is how the Lord sees us—through His eyes of love—even when we are unlovable. "Someone exceedingly precious." That is how He sees us.

Chapter 3

THE COST OF REDEMPTION

HAVING DISCUSSED THE "PEARL OF GREAT PRICE" IN our previous chapter, I want to follow up with an examination of the cost of our redemption. I want to consider the price that Jesus paid.

We have talked about the purchase, and we have talked about the motivation for the purchase. But now, let's go back to the *price*.

HIS OWN BLOOD

In various parts of the New Testament, the price of our redemption is stated very clearly. For now, we will only look at two passages. The first is Acts 20:28, where Paul is talking to the elders of the church at Ephesus:

> *Therefore take heed to yourselves, and to all the flock, among which the Holy Spirit has made you overseers, to shepherd the church of God which He purchased with His own blood.*

Please notice there that Paul gives to Jesus the specific title of *God*. He says God purchased the Church with His own blood. So, the purchase price was *the blood of Jesus.*

The second passage is in First Peter 1, beginning at verse 17:

> *And if you call on the Father, who without partiality judges according to each one's work, conduct yourselves throughout the time of your stay here in fear...*

Some Christians have never heard that verse. Peter is not referring here to a slavish fear, but rather a deep sense of responsibility. What is the reason? It is because of the price that was paid to redeem us. We must never regard ourselves as cheap.

When speaking to young women, I will often quite frankly say, "Never make yourself cheap. You don't have to cheapen yourself to get the right man. Generally speaking, a man will not value you more than you value yourself." The same principle is true for all of us. When you and I realize that we have been redeemed by the blood of Jesus, we cannot afford to make ourselves cheap.

We see the answer for the reason to not cheapen ourselves in verses 18-19:

> ...knowing that you were not redeemed with corruptible [or perishable] things, like silver or gold, from your aimless conduct received by tradition from your fathers, but with the precious blood of Christ, as of a lamb without blemish and without spot.

Please notice again that the price Jesus paid to redeem us is His precious blood. He is called the Lamb of God without blemish and without spot. A blemish, I understand, is something that a creature would be born with. A spot is something that would come upon it afterward. Jesus is without blemish in that He is without original sin.

He is also without spot in that He is without personal sin. It is *His blood* that has redeemed us.

ABUNDANT REDEMPTION

For some added insight on the process of redemption, let's turn to a reference from Psalm 130:7:

> *O Israel, hope in the Lord; for with the Lord there is mercy, and with Him is abundant redemption.*

It is important for us to understand that *redemption* is *buying back*. Where this version says, "abundant redemption," the King James Version said, "plenteous redemption." The New Living Translation says, "His redemption overflows." In light of these phrases, you and I must understand what abundant redemption means. It means that Jesus *overpaid*. He paid *more* than we were worth.

Once when I was preparing a week's worth of Bible teaching for radio on this theme, I wanted to find a good word to describe the love of God that wasn't worn out by religious clichés. After a while, I chose the word *extravagant* because that isn't overused by religious people. Jesus was extravagant. He paid everything. He didn't hold anything back. He actually paid more than the required price.

God's love is extravagant! So many people picture the Lord as being stingy. But He isn't stingy—He is extremely generous. When He sees something He wants, He will pay the full price and more.

HOW JESUS PAID THE PRICE

Let's now consider the way in which Jesus *paid* the price. To begin this section, I want to turn back to an Old Testament preview of the sacrifice of Jesus in Leviticus 16. I believe there are two great prophetic pictures of Jesus and His sacrifice in the Old Testament. Certainly, there are many pictures, but I think the two most significant ones are the Passover lamb and the Day of Atonement. We will study the significance of the Passover in detail in Chapter 7. But in this chapter, I want to look at the Day of Atonement.

THE DAY OF ATONEMENT

The Day of Atonement, which is described in Leviticus 16, is a Jewish holiday that has persisted from then until now. In Hebrew, it is called "Yom Kippur" or "Yom Kippurim," the day of the Hebrew word for *atonement*. Basically, most

Jewish people still fast from sunset until sunset on the next day.

In Jerusalem, it is an absolutely unique day, because all traffic ceases just before sunset and there is no more traffic except for an occasional emergency vehicle. A total silence settles on the city. If you have never experienced something like this, you can hardly imagine what it is like to be in a completely silent city. You can walk out right in the streets, because there is no traffic. No vehicle is going to run you down. Even the non-religious Jews, who are in the majority, are pretty respectful about the Day of Atonement.

In talking about the activities of the Day of Atonement, Leviticus 16:29 gives this mandate from the Lord: "you shall afflict your souls." The Jewish people have always understood that phrase as meaning *to fast*. Many in the Jewish community do fast, going without food or water for 24 hours.

COVERING FOR SIN

Although there are many such observances included in this holy day, I want to focus on the central activity on the Day of Atonement. The essence of this holy day is the high priest going into the Holy of Holies to make atonement for the sins of himself, his household, and the people of Israel. He only did this once a year. It was the only time that any human being went beyond the second veil, out of the holy place into the Holy of Holies. The steps a priest took for the way in were very exactly prescribed. Had any step been varied or missing, the high priest would have died.

Let's read from Leviticus 16, verse 11:

> *And Aaron shall bring the bull of the sin offering, which is for himself, and make atonement for himself and for his house...*

It is important to understand that the Hebrew word in the Old Testament for *atonement* means *covering*. Another form of that same noun is used for the pitch or tar with which Noah and his sons waterproofed the ark. That gives you a picture of the protective covering involved in atonement.

Full atonement was never accomplished in the Old Testament. All that happened was that sin was covered for one more year. This was the case—until Jesus died. Jesus came to put away sin by the sacrifice of Himself. That is one of the key elements which makes the New Covenant totally different from the Old Covenant. After Jesus' death and resurrection, no more sacrifice for sins is required.

INTO HIS PRESENCE

Going back to verses 11-12:

> *...and make atonement for himself and for his house, and shall kill the bull as the sin offering which is for himself. Then he shall take a censer full of burning coals of fire from the altar before the Lord, with his hands full of sweet incense beaten fine, and bring it inside the veil.*

The high priest had to have two elements to get through the veil. He had to have a censer of coals with fragrant incense on it so that a cloud of incense covered him and filled the Holy of Holies. The other item he had to have was the blood of the sacrifice. We see from this picture that entrance into God's presence has to be with *blood* and *incense*.

In a way, I believe this is a pattern for us. It seems to me that we have no right of access into the presence of God unless we come with the incense of worship and the blood of Jesus on our behalf. (We will deal with this subject more fully in Chapter 15.)

The description of the Day of Atonement activity continues in verses 13-14:

> *He shall put the incense on the fire before the Lord, that the cloud of incense may cover the mercy seat that is on the Testimony [that is the copy of the Law that is inside the ark], lest he die. He shall take some of the blood of the bull and sprinkle it with his finger on the mercy seat on the east side; and before the mercy seat he shall sprinkle some of the blood with his finger seven times.*

The tabernacle (and later the temple) faced east, so the east side of the mercy seat was what you would call the front of it. In approaching the mercy seat, making sure that he was at all times enveloped in this cloud of incense, the high priest sprinkled blood seven times in front of the mercy seat. Then he sprinkled it on the front of the mercy seat.

In our next chapter, we will examine how the Day of Atonement relates to Jesus' death and how He too sprinkled His blood seven times before the mercy seat.

Chapter 4

THE SEVENFOLD SPRINKLING

SEVEN IS A VERY SIGNIFICANT NUMBER IN THE BIBLE. IN that regard, I believe the fact that the blood had to be sprinkled seven times before the mercy seat on the Day of Atonement had an exact fulfillment in the experience of Jesus. In this chapter, I will trace with you the sevenfold sprinkling of the blood of Jesus.

The importance of the blood that Jesus shed cannot be diminished. I believe that anyone who does not appreciate the blood of Jesus is soulish and not spiritual. The blood of Jesus is a clear dividing line for Christians. Vast sections of the Church today have turned against the blood of Jesus. One denomination has even published a new hymn book which leaves out every hymn that refers to the blood of Jesus. The blood of Jesus is not only important now—but it will also be a major issue in the years that lie ahead.

In this chapter, as a tribute to the blood Jesus poured out in redeeming us, we will systematically cover the seven separate incidents in which Jesus spilled His blood on our behalf.

THE FIRST SPRINKLING: SWEATING BLOOD

In the Garden of Gethsemane, as Jesus surrendered to the will of the Father in prayer, Luke 22:44 describes the scene in this way:

> *And being in agony, He prayed more earnestly. Then His sweat became like great drops of blood falling down to the ground.*

It wasn't a hot night. Actually, it was probably quite cool, because it was in the springtime. What caused Jesus to break out in profuse sweat? It was the physical, spiritual, and emotional agony that caused Him to sweat, and His blood infused His sweat.

THE SECOND SPRINKLING: BEATEN WITH RODS

For the second event, we come to the scene where Jesus is in the court of Annas, the high priest, as recorded in Matthew 26:67:

> *Then they spat in His face and beat Him; and others struck Him with the palms of their hands.*

If you have a Bible with a marginal reference, it may say regarding the striking that happened "or with rods." Personally, I believe Jesus was struck with rods, because there was a very specific prophecy in the Old Testament foretelling how it would be. Micah 5:1 says:

> *Now gather yourself in troops, O daughter of troops; He has laid siege against us; they will strike the judge of Israel with a rod on the cheek.*

To me, that is a clear prediction of what happened to Jesus. Obviously, if you strike someone with a rod on the cheek, you are certainly going to bring forth blood.

THE THIRD SPRINKLING: SCOURGED

Turning to Matthew 27:26, we see the third incident. This took place upon the final determination of Pontius Pilate as to what to do with Jesus:

> *Then he released Barabbas to them; and when he had scourged Jesus, he delivered Him to be crucified.*

In my opinion, a better translation would be, "when he had Him scourged." Clearly, the governor wasn't going to do the scourging himself.

A Roman scourge was a specialized instrument of torture. It had a handle and various lashes. In the lashes were embedded pieces of bone or metal, placed there deliberately in a design to tear a person's flesh open. That scourging was the third sprinkling of Jesus' blood.

THE FOURTH SPRINKLING: BEARD PLUCKED

The fourth incident goes very closely with Jesus being flogged or scourged. For the detail on the fourth sprinkling, we need to turn back to the Old Testament to the prophet Isaiah. You may or may not have realized that the

New Testament tells us nothing of what went on inside Jesus during His suffering. The New Testament accounts simply present an objective picture of what happened. However, if you read the prophets and the psalms for insights on Jesus' suffering, you will discover many details about what Jesus endured within Himself.

The spirit of the Messiah predicted what would be His own sufferings in the Old Testament. Indeed, the prophets spoke in the first person about events that didn't happen to them, but to the suffering servant. Here is one very clear example in Isaiah 50:6:

> *I gave My back to those who struck Me [that is the flogging]...*

Please notice that He *gave* His back. Jesus offered His back by His own free will and choice. It is very important to understand this truth—He did not struggle. He did not resist. He did not protest.

> *...and My cheeks to those who plucked out the beard; I did not hide My face from shame and spitting.*

This prophetic picture means that among the abusive actions used toward Jesus, they also roughly pulled out hairs from His beard. In the process of doing so, it is very likely they brought forth blood by that action.

THE FIFTH SPRINKLING: CROWN OF THORNS

For the fifth incident, we turn to Matthew 27, verse 28, where the Roman soldiers are mocking Jesus:

> *And they stripped Him and put a scarlet [or purple] robe on Him.*

Probably, the use of the word *purple* would be better here, because it was the color of royalty. The soldiers were mocking Him and saying, "If you're a king, let's give you a king's clothing." First of all, they gave Him this purple robe, which must then have been stained with His own blood. Then they gave Him a crown—but it was a crown of thorns.

Just for a moment, I want to give you another aspect of the perfectness of the atonement of Jesus. He not only atoned for the human race, He also atoned for all the consequences that man's sin had brought upon the earth. Any way you look at this fulfillment, it is perfect.

In Genesis, God had said to Adam when he sinned, "From now on, the earth will bring forth thorns and thistles." The thistle is purple, the same color as the robe Jesus was clothed with. The thorns were real thorns. If you were to visit Jerusalem today, someone could show you the type of thorns that were used for the crown. They were very long spikes, very hard—almost as hard as nails, and extremely sharp.

So, having put the purple robe on Him, they then crowned Him with thorns. We read what happened next in verses 28-30:

> *And they stripped Him and put a [purple] robe on Him. When they had twisted a crown of thorns, they put it on His head, and a reed in His right hand [that was His scepter]. And they bowed the knee before Him and mocked Him, saying, "Hail, King of the Jews!" Then they spat on Him, and took the reed and struck Him on the head.*

Both with the reed and most probably with their hands as well, they pressed those thorns right down into His scalp. It is commonly known that the scalp, when it is penetrated, bleeds very freely. To our mind comes the picture of Jesus with huge tufts of His beard pulled out, the marks from the beating with rods on His cheeks, the blood flowing down from His scalp on every side, coagulating in His remaining beard. Scripture says in Isaiah 52:14: "...so His visage [appearance] was marred more than any man, and His form more than the sons of men." The more literal translation of this verse would be: "He lost the very appearance of man." After what Jesus had endured, He no longer looked human.

So that was the fifth shedding of blood—the crown of thorns.

THE SIXTH SPRINKLING: CRUCIFIXION

For the sixth incident, we come to the actual crucifixion, which is described in Matthew 27:35. Remarkably, it is said in just three words. Really, that is amazing. Any modern writer would have expounded for paragraphs on all that happened. But all the Bible says is, "They crucified Him." We know the wounds inflicted by the practice of crucifixion, and also from what Jesus said after His resurrection, inviting His disciples to look at the marks of the crucifixion. We know that His executioners pierced both His hands and His feet. Again, His blood came out profusely—especially, I believe, from His hands.

Generally speaking, present-day scholars don't believe that they pierced the palms of His hands, but on the wrists between the radius and ulna bones instead. This is because, medically speaking, it would be very difficult for Him to bear the weight of His body with only the palms of His hands. But if the nails went in on the upper side of the wrist, apparently there is strength in the carpels, or wrist bones, to support the weight. This piercing of His hands and feet was the sixth sprinkling of His blood.

THE SEVENTH SPRINKLING: THE SPEAR

For the seventh and final sprinkling of Jesus' blood, we will refer to John 19, the stage at which Jesus had already expired on the cross. Then, John 19:31 says:

> *Therefore, because it was the Preparation Day, that the bodies should not remain on the cross on the Sabbath (for that Sabbath was a high day [or a high holiday]), the Jews asked Pilate that their legs might be broken, and that they might be taken away.*

If a person who was being crucified had not yet died, the executioners would bring on death more quickly by breaking the legs. This would swiftly cause death because, in order to keep breathing, a person had to raise his body up with his legs. If the legs were broken, the person couldn't raise himself up and would die of asphyxiation.

The account continues on with verses 32-33:

> *Then the soldiers came and broke the legs of the first and of the other who was crucified with Him [those were the two thieves]. But when they came to Jesus and saw that He was already dead, they did not break His legs.*

Jesus did not actually die of the physical effects of crucifixion. Rather, He died of a broken heart brought on by rejection. Verse 34 says:

> *But one of the soldiers pierced His side with a spear, and immediately blood and water came out.*

The "water" was apparently the pericardial fluid, which was released by the spear. Reading a little further, we see another illustration of the total exactness of what happened in Jesus' sacrifice on the cross. Verses 35-36 continue:

> *And he who has seen [that is the apostle John] has testified, and his testimony is true; and he*

knows that he is telling the truth, so that you may believe. For these things were done [now notice the next phrase:] that the Scripture should be fulfilled....

Everything that happened to Jesus was the fulfillment of God's predetermined counsel revealed in Scripture. God never lost control of the situation for one moment.

...the Scripture should be fulfilled, "Not one of His bones shall be broken" [see Numbers 9:12 and Psalm 34:20].

That phrase, "Not one of His bones shall be broken," is stated about the Passover lamb. In spite of all the cruelties and abuse that Jesus endured, none of His bones were broken.

And again another Scripture says, "They shall look on Him whom they pierced" (John 19:37).

Can you see from this how every single detail ordained by God was exactly implemented, even though it was wicked, godless men who carried it out? It is so important for you and me to realize that we are not called upon to go through all that Jesus went through. Even so, at times most of us are subjected to the forces of evil, to unfair treatment, and maybe even to brutality. It is good for us to be reminded that no one can do anything more than God will allow. He is in ultimate control.

This is the conclusion of our examination of the seven-fold sprinkling of the blood of Jesus. As far as I understand (and this is an area where it is not always easy to be certain), the sprinkling of blood on the mercy seat took place later. We will come to that discussion a little further along in the course of this study, when we learn about our way of access into the Holy of Holies in Chapter 15.

Chapter 5

LIFE IS IN
THE BLOOD

THERE IS MORE THAT WE NEED TO UNDERSTAND ABOUT
the importance of Jesus shedding His blood seven times
in the Passion. In this chapter, I want to examine two
passages in the Old Testament that will help us to understand the full implications of the shedding of Jesus' blood.

ABSTAINING FROM BLOOD

The first truth is found in Leviticus chapter 17. It would
be easy to say that Leviticus is a rather dull book. But in
the midst of this book, there are the most marvelous jewels of truth.

As I see it, one strong theme of Leviticus is that God's people must not at any time partake of the blood of any animal they eat. That admonition still applies to Christians. Do you realize that? We need to be aware of this prohibition, because there is a great deal of ignorance on this subject.

In Acts 15, the early church, which was exclusively Jewish, had to face the problem of what to do with Gentiles who were believing in Jesus. There was one faction that said, "Well, they have got to come under the law of Moses, be circumcised, keep the Law, and become like Jews. Then they can be saved." But Paul and Barnabas, as well as Peter and James, took their stand against this faction. They said, "No, that isn't necessary." Peter said, in effect, "We Jews couldn't observe the Law and keep it. Why should we try to make the Gentiles observe something we couldn't observe?"

Although we would do well to examine the whole discussion recorded in Acts, here was the final determination of the council at the end in Acts 15:28-29:

For it seemed good to the Holy Spirit, and to us...

By the way, that *is* the kind of decision we need to arrive at in the Church—where it seems good to the Holy Spirit and to us. Sometimes we leave the Holy Spirit out.

> ...*to lay upon you [Gentiles] no greater burden than these necessary things [What are they?]: that you abstain from things offered to idols, from blood, from things strangled, and from sexual immorality.*

There are four prohibitions stated:

1. Things offered to idols.

2. Eating blood.

3. Things strangled. (Why things strangled? Because if a thing is strangled, the blood remains in it.)

4. Sexual immorality.

You will notice that partaking of blood is put in the same category with sexual immorality. Clearly, our standards are not always the same as God's. In some parts of the world, people eat what they call blood pudding. As I understand it, that is absolutely forbidden for Christians. Eating blood is just the same, in God's sight, as immorality.

LIFE BLOOD

Having seen the current, up-to-date importance of abstaining from blood, let's continue our study of Leviticus 17, dealing with the issue of not partaking of the blood. We see various scriptural regulations given about avoiding this practice, along with the reasons behind them.

In verse 10 of Leviticus 17, the Lord says through Moses:

> *And whatever man of the house of Israel, or of the strangers who dwell among you, who eats any blood, I will set My face against that person who eats blood, and will cut him off from among his people.*

In verse 11, the Lord gives the reason, and this reason is also one of the most wonderful prophecies of the Bible:

> *For the life of the flesh is in the blood [now note carefully], and I have given it to you upon the altar to make atonement for your souls.*

Where it says, "the life of the flesh," the Hebrew says, "the soul [Hebrew *nephesh*] of the flesh." So, it is the soul-life that is in the blood. This is a confirmation of what we know—when the blood ceases to circulate, there is no more life in the body.

At first, the scriptural mandate sounds simply like a regulation: you are going to use the blood to make atonement, therefore you do not partake of it. But it is also prophetic, because the Lord is speaking. He says, "I have given it to you upon the altar [of the cross] to make atonement for your souls...."

On the cross, Jesus gave His soul-life, which was in His blood, as the redemption price for our souls. This follows the pattern of the law of redemption, which is an eye for an eye, a tooth for a tooth, burning for burning, beating for beating, soul for soul. On the cross, Jesus gave His soul to redeem every soul of humanity.

THE PATHWAY OF HUMILITY

Let's look for a moment at the last verses of Isaiah 52, which are the introduction to the great atonement chapter in Isaiah 53. Verse 13 of Isaiah 52 is the introduction to the Servant of the Lord, the Suffering Servant, and it says:

> *Behold, My Servant shall deal prudently [He shall carry out the whole will of God]; He shall be exalted and extolled and be very high.*

In like manner, Philippians 2:9 says:

> *Therefore God also has highly exalted Him and given Him the name which is above every name.*

I find it amazing that *before* Jesus' humiliation is depicted in Isaiah 53, the Word of God promises His ultimate exaltation at the end of Isaiah chapter 52.

THE STAIRWAY OF HUMILITY

This pathway of humility and ensuing honor and glory is beautifully described in Philippians 2, beginning in verse 5:

> *Let this mind be in you [learn to think the way that Jesus thought] which was also in Christ Jesus...*

Here is the sevenfold humiliation Jesus underwent:

> *...who, being in the form of God, did not consider it robbery to be equal with God...*

A better translation might be: "did not consider equality with God something to be grasped at." He had it by divine, eternal right—so He didn't need to grasp at it.

...but made Himself of no reputation...

The Greek says, literally, *He emptied Himself.* One of Charles Wesley's hymns, "And Can It Be," says, "He emptied Himself of all but love."

...taking the form of a bondservant...

That is the second step down. Though He was the Son of God, Jesus became a servant, "coming in the likeness of men." He came down to the level of man, which is a little lower than the angels.

And being found in the appearance as a man,

He was nothing special. He was just an ordinary man, the carpenter's son.

He humbled Himself...

He became a humble man. He wasn't a priest or a ruler. He was a working man. Years ago, I heard a preacher who prayed to the Lord and asked, "Lord, show me Your hands." The Lord answered and gave him a vision of His hands. He expected to see the nail prints in the hands, but he didn't. He saw the hands of an ordinary working man, and that really impressed him. Jesus was a humble, ordinary man.

...and [He] became obedient to...death...

That is the sixth step down. The ultimate step down is:

...the death of the cross.

To summarize those steps downward, we could put it as follows:

1. **Emptied Himself.**

2. **A servant**: Though He was the Son of God.

3. **Coming in the likeness of men**: He was in human form, but He could have been in Adamic perfection.

4. **Human appearance**: When Peter said, "You are the Christ." Jesus replied, "Flesh and blood has not revealed this to you." There was nothing in His outward appearance to indicate who He was.

5. **A humble Man**: Just a carpenter's son. Not in any way disparaging carpenters. Jesus was a working man.

6. **Obedient to death**: He could have died on a sick bed, but He didn't.

7. **Death on a cross**: The death of a criminal, in agony and shame.

These are the seven steps down. But Paul then follows them with the seven steps up. Can you see how perfect the structure of the Bible is? You have to remember that these were just written as letters. Paul didn't sit down and have a theological scheme. He may not have even made an outline. But the Holy Spirit guided him with total exactness.

STAIRWAY TO GLORY

Please notice that there is a very important word in Philippians 2, verse 9: *"Therefore."* Because of what? Because Jesus humbled Himself. You see, Jesus Himself said, "For whoever exalts himself will be humbled, and he who humbles himself will be exalted." That truth applies to everybody.

The two clearest examples of this principle are Jesus and Satan. Satan (who was originally Lucifer) exalted himself, reaching up for something he wasn't entitled to, and fell. Jesus, on the other hand, was entitled to a position of equality with God, voluntarily renounced it, and went down—only to be raised up in glory.

Here is the *therefore*—it signifies the result of His humbling Himself. Jesus didn't receive the position He has in the universe as a favorite Son; He earned it. He qualified for it. How? By humbling Himself.

Let's now look at the seven steps up in the experience of Jesus.

> *Therefore God also has highly exalted Him...*

If you turn back to Isaiah 52:13, you find, "He shall be exalted and extolled and be very high." I think the rabbis interpret that: "He will be made higher than Abraham, higher than Moses, and higher than the angels." Returning to Philippians 2:9:

> *...and given Him the name which is above every name...*

Notice it is "the" name. The King James Version says "a name." But the real translation is "the name." The one name that is above every name.

> *That at the name of Jesus every knee should bow, of those in heaven, and of those on earth, and of*

those under the earth, and that every tongue should confess that Jesus Christ [the Messiah] is Lord, to the glory of God the Father.

Here then, is the summary of Jesus' exaltation.

1. Highly exalted.
2. The Name above every name.
3. Every knee shall bow at His name.
4. Those in heaven.
5. Those on earth.
6. Those under the earth.
7. Every tongue shall confess.

Do you see how perfect that structure is? Seven steps down and seven steps up.

AN OFFERING FOR SIN

Let's move on now to Isaiah 53, verse 12, which is exactly in line with Leviticus 17:11—the verse which says: "the soul of all flesh is in the blood." Isaiah 53:12 says:

Therefore I will divide Him a portion with the great, and He shall divide the spoil with the strong, because He poured out His soul unto death...

How did He pour out His soul unto death? Through what? His blood. It was through His blood that He gave His soul. I truly believe that Jesus gave the last drop of His blood—He gave His whole soul as the one, final, all-sufficient sin offering for the world.

Isaiah 53:10 says:

> *Yet it pleased the Lord [Father] to bruise Him;*
> *He has put Him to grief. When You make His*
> *soul an offering for sin...*

Another translation of that concept would be, "when His soul makes a sin offering." His soul was the ultimate sin offering and He poured out His soul in His blood.

I hope you can see how precise the Bible is, how very exact. Every part of it fits together. No human mind could ever have devised such a work. Something written by Moses, something written by Isaiah, and something written by Paul are in complete agreement—writers who are separated by centuries. In my opinion, in light of its exactness, I think it is silly *not* to believe the Bible. Many people who disregard the Word of God think they are clever, but they are really foolish.

In the next chapter, we will go on to learn how we can appropriate the shed blood of Jesus for ourselves.

Chapter 6

HOW TO
APPROPRIATE
THE BLOOD

As we consider how to appropriate what has been provided for us through the shed blood of Jesus, I want to highlight one of my favorite passages, Revelation 12:11:

> *And they [the believers on earth] overcame him [Satan] by the blood of the Lamb and by the word of their testimony, and they did not love their lives to the death.*

Only people who have lost their lives qualify for this category of overcomers. You remember the steps for following

Jesus described in Luke 9:23? Deny yourself and take up your cross daily. Lay down your life and find a new life. The people to whom John refers in Revelation 12:11 are those who have done exactly this. By giving up their lives, they qualify to defeat Satan.

Satan is not the least bit frightened of uncommitted Christians who can pray and use all sorts of spiritual words in their preaching. They don't really have any impact on Satan. The only people he is frightened of are the committed Christians who have laid down their lives.

When the Bible says, "They did not love their lives to the death," it means that, for them, staying alive was *not* their number-one priority. Priority number one for them was to do the will of God, whether they lived or not. Their most important obligation was to be faithful to the Lord.

CASTING SATAN FROM THE HEAVENS

The verse that follows Revelation 12:11 brings forth an interesting revelation:

> *Therefore rejoice, O heavens, and you who dwell in them! Woe to the inhabitants of the earth and the sea! For the devil has come down to you, having great wrath, because he knows that he has a short time.*

A *free* Derek Prince resource for you!

To further introduce you to the unique ministry of one of the great Bible teachers of our time, Derek Prince Ministries would like to send you one of his most acclaimed, timeless teachings.

Derek Prince's message on audio CD entitled "Do You Realize How Valuable You Are?" has helped countless people around the world discover the freedom, power and purpose that flow from a revelation of your worth to your heavenly Father. Simply fill out and return this card, and we'll get it right out to you!

☐ **Yes,** please send me the Derek Prince teaching "Do You Realize How Valuable You Are?" on audio CD. CD4411

name: _____

address: _____

city: _____ state: _____ zip: _____

e-mail: _____

www.derekprince.org   ![f] www.facebook.com/dpmlegacy   ![twitter] @DPMUSA

![instagram] youtube.com/DerekPrinceMinistry    pinterest.com/derekprinceusa

BUSINESS REPLY MAIL

FIRST-CLASS MAIL   PERMIT NO 705   CHARLOTTE NC

POSTAGE WILL BE PAID BY ADDRESSEE

DEREK PRINCE MINISTRIES
PO BOX 19501
CHARLOTTE NC 28219-9932

At the point described in this verse, heaven has been purged—"rejoice, O heavens." But look out earth! Why? Because now the devil isn't in heaven any longer. He is right down on earth. He has come to earth knowing he has only got a few short years to do all the mischief and make all the harm that he can.

A BRIEF PERIOD

To me, it is clear that the period the devil has on earth is closely related to the seventy-weeks prophecy of Daniel Chapter 9. Whether it is a whole week or half the week, I am not prepared to offer an opinion. But it is clear that in Revelation 12:12 we have come to a specific period of time. The devil, who is a student of prophecy, knows it pretty well. When he comes down out of heaven onto the earth, he knows he has three and a half years to do his mischief.

Jesus says in Mark 13:20, "And unless the Lord had shortened those days, no flesh would be saved; but for the elect's sake, whom He chose, He shortened the days." Though theoretically it is three and a half years, there are going to be at least a few days taken off at the end. However, the devil is going to exert himself to do the maximum amount of harm in that short period of time before he is bound and imprisoned in the bottomless pit.

If we look back to Revelation 12:11, we learn that the believers on earth overcome Satan by the blood of the Lamb and by the word of their testimony. Do you see that it is the believer on earth who eventually gets the devil down out of heaven? It is not so much the angels. They have their part to play, as they did with Daniel. But ultimately, it is the believers on earth who procure the final defeat in the casting down of Satan.

Doesn't that make you feel good? I think it is tremendous. But here is something very important for us to realize. The devil wants to keep you ignorant about the vital role you will play. As long as he keeps believers unaware, they will not do what God has appointed them to do. So, the devil fights by every means in his power to keep us oblivious to this one fact: that God has given us the spiritual weapons that can cast down Satan from his place in the heavenlies.

Before we move on into more detail, we need to be reminded of this Scripture from Second Corinthians 10:4-5:

> *For the weapons of our warfare are not carnal but mighty in God for pulling down strongholds, casting down arguments and every high*

thing that exalts itself against the knowledge of God...

The spiritual weapons given to us will enable us to cast down every high thing that opposes God and His kingdom. The last, the ultimate, the supreme high thing that opposes God is Satan's kingdom in the heavenlies. Amazingly, God has committed to us the weapons that will enable us to do it.

THE LORD'S ARMY

Christians regularly talk about being soldiers in the Lord's army. But many of us have a very vague and rather sentimental idea about what it is to be a soldier. As I mentioned, by no choice of my own, I was a soldier in the British Army in World War II for over five years. When I was conscripted, I did not get a nice little certificate from the commanding officer saying, "We guarantee that you'll never have to lose your life." No soldier has ever joined an army on the condition that he will not be killed. In fact, in a certain sense, any time a soldier joins an army, one of the prerequisites is affirming the possibility that he or she may be killed.

It is the same in the Lord's army. You and I have no guarantee that we will not have to lay down our lives. The people Satan fears are those who are not afraid to lay down their lives. After all, life is comparatively brief. It is not going to go on forever. It would be foolish to miss eternal glory for the sake of a few brief years on earth.

TOTAL COMMITMENT

The people mentioned in Revelation 12:11 were people totally committed to God. Whether they lived or whether they died was not important to them. What was important to them was that they should fulfill their God-appointed function to overthrow Satan and cast him down.

I believe it is enlightened self-interest to have this realigned sense of value—this embracing of what is more important. This wonderful statement in First John affirms that perspective:

> *The world and its desires pass away, but whoever does the will of God lives forever* (1 John 2:17 NIV).

When you unite your will in total commitment with the will of God, you become unsinkable. You are undefeatable. You are unshakable. Whether you live or whether you die is of secondary importance. Whatever happens, you cannot be defeated.

I want to share another insight from Revelation 12:11 that I believe the Lord showed me. It came in answer to this question: How do we overcome Satan? Many people know it is by the blood of the Lamb and by the word of our testimony. But they tend to make it a repetitive phrase like, "I plead the blood... I plead the blood... I plead the blood..." I don't want to underestimate that activity, but I have observed that sometimes doing that doesn't impress the devil. I think we have to apply the truth of this practice more intelligently.

OVERCOMING SATAN

How do we overcome Satan? By the blood of the Lamb and by the word of our testimony. As I understand it, there are three elements in this passage—the blood, the Word (which is the Word of God), and our testimony.

Here is the key. Testify personally to what the Word says that the blood does for you. Please let me say that again. *This is how you overcome Satan: by the blood of the Lamb, and by the word of your testimony.* The key words are *testimony, word,* and *blood*. So, you testify personally to what the Word (that's the Scripture) says that the blood does for you. In other words, to make it effective, you must make it personal.

To whom are you testifying? To *Satan*. This is not a believer's testimony meeting where we share the story of God's grace in our lives. This takes place when you and I come face to face with the enemy of our souls. We speak directly to him in the name and the authority of the Lord Jesus Christ, and we tell the devil what the Word of God says the blood of Jesus does for us.

It should be obvious that for you and I to be able to do that, we must know what the Word says about the blood. If you do not know that, you cannot exercise this weapon. In fact, as long as you remain ignorant of the Word of God, ultimately you will become prey to the devil. The great weapon of attack is the sword of the Spirit, which is the Word of God. The Scripture says it is your responsibility and mine to take it. Ephesians 6:17 says: "take...the sword of the Spirit, which is the word of God."

Here is what we must understand. You and I have to take the blood from (if you like) the "blood bank" and get it into our lives. In the following two chapters, I would like to take a look at the Passover ceremony to see just how we can take the blood and apply it to our lives.

Chapter 7

THE PASSOVER CEREMONY

In our previous chapter, we learned from Revelation 12:11 how to practically appropriate the blood of Jesus. In learning further about how to apply the blood to our lives, the Passover ceremony provides an excellent parallel to help our understanding.

Let's turn our attention to Exodus 12, because this chapter records the ordinance of the Passover. You will remember that the Passover was God's provision of deliverance and salvation for Israel in Egypt. Each family had to take a lamb (the father, incidentally, and no one else in the family could do it)—the father had to kill or sacrifice the lamb and catch its blood in a basin. This process of sacrificing the lamb is a tremendous demonstration to me of the responsibility of fathers as priests of their families. Every father had to act as the priest in his family.

THE SIGNIFICANCE OF HYSSOP

Once the lamb had been killed and its blood had been caught in the basin, there was another step. The blood was very precious and none of it was to be spilled to the ground. But the blood *in the basin* didn't protect any Israelite family. The fathers had to get the blood from the basin to the place *where they lived*. How did those fathers do it? The following passage tells us what they did:

> *Then Moses called for all the elders of Israel and said to them, "Pick out and take lambs for yourselves according to your families, and kill the Passover lamb. And you shall take a bunch of hyssop, dip it in the blood that is in the basin, and strike the lintel and the two doorposts with the blood that is in the basin. And none of you shall go out of the door of his house until morning. For the Lord will pass through to strike the Egyptians; and when He sees the*

*blood on the lintel and on the two doorposts,
the Lord will pass over [that is the Hebrew
word pessach, which means pass over. Hence
the name Passover.] the door and not allow the
destroyer to come into your houses to strike you"*
(Exodus 12:21-23).

There are two important regulations in this passage.
First of all, they had to get the blood from the basin to
where they lived. There was only one means stipulated to
do that, and that means was *hyssop*. You may know that
hyssop is a very common plant that grows all over the
Middle East, almost like a weed. There is no problem find-
ing hyssop. The fathers had to pick a bunch of the hyssop,
dip it in the blood, and strike it on the lintels (the top and
two sides), but never on the threshold. You are *never* to
walk over the blood.

Once the blood had been transferred from the basin to
the place where they lived, they were safe on one condition: What was that? *They had to stay inside the house.* You
see, this is very important—the blood *only* protects the
obedient. You are safe while you obey.

HIGH PRIEST OF OUR CONFESSION

I cannot overemphasize the importance of your testimony. The book of Hebrews reinforces this point:

> *Therefore, holy brethren, partakers of the heavenly calling, consider the Apostle and High Priest of our confession, Christ Jesus* (Hebrews 3:1).

The writer of Hebrews calls Jesus the "High Priest of our confession." *Confession* means literally *saying the same as*. For us as believers in the Bible and in Jesus Christ, confession means we say the same with our mouths that God says in His Word. We make the words of our mouth agree with the Word of God. Jesus is the High Priest of *our confession*. If we have no confession, then we have no High Priest.

SETTLING OUR DESTINY

Without a conscious, intentional agreement with God's Word, Jesus cannot represent you before God. He can only advocate on your behalf when you make the right confession. In the gospel of Matthew, Jesus said, "For by your words you will be justified, and by your words you will be condemned" (Matt. 12:37). You settle your destiny by the words you speak.

James said the tongue is like the rudder on a ship. It is a very small part of the ship, but it determines exactly where the ship will go (James 3:4). Likewise, we determine the course of our lives by the way we use our tongues. Many Christians are very careless and delinquent in the way they use their tongues: "I'm dying to see you." "I was tickled to death." "I was so embarrassed, I just wanted to die." Generally, I believe it would be wise never to say anything about yourself that you would not want Jesus to make happen.

Be very careful not to sell yourself short, because God holds you in very high regard. He invested the blood of Jesus in you. When you use your own tongue to criticize yourself, what you are really doing is criticizing God's handiwork. In Ephesians, Paul says we are His workmanship or masterpiece (see Eph. 2:10). I believe it is dangerously presumptuous to criticize the workmanship of God. Pride, of course, is rampant among Christians. But another problem that is just as great is underestimating ourselves.

OBEDIENCE *BEFORE* SPRINKLING

In First Peter 1:1-2, we read Peter's greeting:

> *To the pilgrims of the Dispersion...*

The Greek word is *diaspora*. It is specifically addressed to the Jews outside the land of Israel, which is still the normal Jewish way of describing them today, the *diaspora*.

> *...in Pontus, Galatia, Cappadocia, Asia, and Bithynia, elect [or chosen] according to the foreknowledge of God the Father, in [or through] sanctification of the Spirit, for [but I prefer the old translation, "unto"] obedience and sprinkling of the blood of Jesus Christ....*

Notice, *obedience* comes before *sprinkling*. The blood is *not* sprinkled on the disobedient. The blood does not protect those who go out of the house. It only protects those who are behind it or covered by it.

APPLYING THE BLOOD

Here is the burning question for Israel and for us: *How do we get the shed blood—since the sacrifice is complete— to the place where we live?* As long as we just look at the blood in the basin, it is not going to do us any good. The blood is available, but it does nothing. We have to take this simple little plant called hyssop, dip it in the blood, and strike it on the outside of our house over the door. Then we are protected.

A further application of the teaching of the Passover and the Feast of Unleavened Bread to Christians comes to us from Paul in First Corinthians 5:7:

Therefore purge out the old leaven...

That phrase refers to the Feast of Unleavened Bread. At that feast time, every Jewish family had to eliminate everything that was leavened from their house for seven days. Some of them still do it today.

...that you may be a new lump, since you truly are unleavened...

Verse 8 continues:

Therefore let us keep the feast, not with old leaven, nor with the leaven of malice and wickedness [that is the old leaven—malice and wickedness], but with the unleavened bread of sincerity and truth.

That is the spiritual application connected to the Passover. But first we need to go back to the end of verse 7 for an important link that cannot be left out:

> *For indeed Christ [or the Messiah], our Passover,*
> *was sacrificed for us.*

Can you see the very clear link of the Passover to the sacrifice of Jesus on the Cross? Peter explains further:

> *Knowing that you were not redeemed with*
> *corruptible things, like silver or gold, from your*
> *aimless conduct received by tradition from your*
> *fathers, but with the precious blood of Christ,*
> *as of a lamb without blemish and without spot*
> (1 Peter 1:18-19).

Please notice Peter's use of the word *lamb*. This again takes us back to the Passover. In Chapter 8 we will begin to see how we can use what we have learned about the Passover and apply it in our own lives.

Chapter 8

A PERSONAL APPLICATION

IN THIS CHAPTER, WE WANT TO EXPLORE THE PERSONAL application of what we have been learning. Without question, we can say that the Passover Lamb was killed more than nineteen centuries ago. In a manner of speaking, the blood is in the basin. Jesus' blood has been shed for us, but the blood in the basin doesn't protect us. We have to transfer the blood from the basin to where we live.

THE HYSSOP IS OUR TESTIMONY

Under the Old Covenant, we used *hyssop* to transfer the blood. But that is not what we use under the New

Covenant. What do we use under the new? The answer is *our testimony*. It is our personal testimony that takes the blood out of the basin and applies it to our lives, to our situation, to our family, and to the place where we live.

Do you remember what we learned from Revelation 12:11? We could paraphrase it to say: "We overcome Satan when we use the hyssop." What is the hyssop? It is our personal testimony. "We overcome Satan when we testify personally to what the Word of God says the blood does for us." That action takes the blood from the basin and sprinkles it upon ourselves, upon our lives, upon any situation where it is legitimate to apply it.

I would like to invite you to do this personally. It is your opportunity to appropriate the blood of Jesus into your life. Of all the truths I have learned from the Bible, if I had to choose one that is the most valuable and the most powerful, this would be it. You see, we didn't really deal with the full significance of the statement we studied that Jesus "poured out His soul unto death." In the blood of Jesus, there was God's own life. It is the life of the One who created the whole universe—infinitely more powerful than anything He created. In the light of this truth there is no way the human mind can ever measure the power that was released in the blood of Jesus.

ONE DROP

Years ago, when I was preaching in Zambia, I said, "There is more power in one drop of the blood of Jesus than there is in all the kingdom of Satan." For brother Mahesh Chavda, who was with me, that statement ignited something in his spirit. He went on from Zambia to Zaire (now Democratic Republic of Congo) to preach for a week in the capital. In Kinshasa, God moved in such a way that the crowds in that city grew in one week from 50,000 to 350,000 people. Many miracles took place, including a young boy who was raised from the dead. He had been in the hospital for several hours when he came back to life. But Mahesh said to me afterward, "The truth that gave me the faith was that one statement: 'There is more power in one drop of the blood of Jesus than there is in the whole kingdom of Satan.'"

Unfortunately, it has become somewhat fashionable, in a way, to downplay the blood of Jesus—even for people who theoretically believe in it. I think some Christians tend to bow to academic prejudices. If people want to be considered knowledgeable, they don't talk too much about the blood of Jesus because that is regarded as primitive.

I heard a preacher once say, "All that was accomplished for us by the blood of Jesus was negative." I *totally* disagree! The most positive thing in the universe is the life of God, and that life is released through the blood of Jesus.

You and I can learn how to appropriate what is in the blood of Jesus, the very life of God. There is nothing we will ever need that isn't in it. How do we appropriate it? We overcome Satan when we testify personally to what the Word says the blood does for us. It has to be personal. If you believe this truth, I would like you to say this phrase out loud right now:

> *We overcome Satan when we testify personally to what the Word says the blood does for us.*

Praise the Lord!

Chapter 9

REDEMPTION

LET'S RETURN NOW TO THE SCRIPTURE THAT WE HAVE
been exploring for the last few chapters, which is
Revelation 12:11:

> *They overcame him by the blood of the Lamb,*
> *and by the word of their testimony; and they did*
> *not love their lives [their souls] to the death.*

The conclusion we reached is that you and I can make a
practical application out of that statement in this way: *We*
overcome Satan when we testify personally to what the Word
says the blood does for us. There are three elements in that
statement: the Word, the blood, and our testimony. Our

testimony is the hyssop that transfers the blood from the basin to the place where we live.

POWER OF THE BLOOD

In the next seven chapters, we are going to work through what I have termed the seven-fold power of the blood. We will explore seven specific ways we can apply the blood of Jesus in our own lives as revealed in the Scriptures. I personally believe these seven are definitive. In a way, when you have them, you have the central truth about the blood. Not only was the blood sprinkled seven times, but it works seven ways.

My goal in the coming chapters is to *teach* you what the blood does according to the Word of God. Unless you and I know what the Word teaches about the blood, we can't testify. We *have* to be familiar with the Word.

In this chapter, we will explore the first application, which is *redemption*. *To redeem* means *to buy back*. We had sold ourselves by our sin to Satan and were exposed for sale in Satan's slave market. Jesus walked into the market and paid the price to buy us back out of the hand of Satan. That is redemption.

BEING IN CHRIST

For our further understanding of redemption, let's take a look at Ephesians 1:7. This is one of Paul's immensely long sentences, so we will not cover all of it—only the parts that apply to redemption.

> *In Him [that is Jesus] we have redemption through His blood, the forgiveness of sins, according to the riches of His grace...*

We have redemption through the blood of Jesus—when we are in Christ. Do you understand the implication? We have to be *in Christ* to have the redemption. Another benefit purchased for us by the blood of Jesus is the forgiveness of our sins. Compare what Jesus said at the Last Supper in Matthew 26:28 as He gave them the cup, which was the emblem of His blood. He said:

> *For this is My blood of the new covenant, which is shed for many for the remission [or forgiveness] of sins.*

Similarly, Hebrews 9:22 says, "without shedding of blood there is no remission of sin." So, the blood of Jesus was shed that our sins might be forgiven.

THE REQUIREMENT OF FORGIVENESS

You will notice in the portion of Ephesians 1:7 quoted above that Paul makes these two truths coextensive—redemption through His blood and the forgiveness of sins. It is very important for us to understand that we only have the full legal rights of redemption insofar as our sins are forgiven. If *all* our sins are forgiven, we have the *total* rights of redemption. But if there is any sin in our life—unconfessed and unforgiven—in that area we do not have the full legal rights of redemption. Satan still has a claim in that area.

We have seen the direct outworking of this truth many times in the ministry of deliverance. If Satan has a legitimate claim, he will not give it up. You can shout in his face, you can fast for a week, you can do all that is possible to bring freedom. But the situation will not change, and the enemy will remain—because he knows he has a legal claim that still has not been settled in that area.

FAILURE TO FORGIVE

Another very common related area by which believers give Satan a legal claim to remain in their lives is their failure to forgive others. In the Lord's Prayer, Jesus has taught us that we are forgiven of God in the same measure in which we forgive others: "Forgive us our sins, as we forgive those who sin against us" (Matt. 6:12 NLT).

We are not entitled to claim forgiveness from God above the measure in which we forgive others. Therefore, if there is any person whom we do *not* forgive, in that measure correspondingly we are *not* forgiven of God. Consequently, that area of unforgiveness in our own lives is an area where Satan still has a legal claim. Do what you will, you cannot dislodge him until you have forgiven whoever it may be that you need to forgive.

You can get all the preachers in your country to preach at you and pray for you. But you won't dislodge the devil, because he knows he has a legal claim. One fact you need to remember about the devil is this: he's a legal expert and he knows it. However, God's Word offers us total forgiveness of sin. It is most important that we hold on to the total forgiveness and that we don't leave anything unforgiven.

STIRRING UP THE DEVIL

One of the great ministries of the Holy Spirit through the Word is to cause the devil to get stirred up at us. Many people have said to me, "I had a much more peaceful time before I was baptized in the Holy Spirit." That is not surprising, because if you have evil spirits in you that are not driven out, then there will be a conflict that was never there before. The Holy Spirit will force the enemy out into the open.

That is precisely why some people don't like Holy Spirit-focused religion. Why? Because they would rather keep the enemy suppressed and respectable than have him forced out into the open and behave like the beast he really is. They would rather keep up the religious façade and remain respectable in front of their neighbors than be heard burping, or spitting, or screaming as the Holy Spirit moves in them to force the enemy out into the open.

I always tell people in a deliverance service that they will come to a place where they may have to make a choice between their dignity on one hand and their deliverance on the other. My advice has always been to let dignity go and choose deliverance, because your dignity will come back later. But if you hold on to your dignity, all you are doing is covering over the presence of the enemy in your life.

Quite frankly, the devil is glad to be suppressed rather than to be driven out. Given the choice, that is what he prefers. But the way to stir him up—the way to get him so mad he just can't keep quiet any longer—is testify about the blood of Jesus. When that happens, the devil's devices begin to show themselves for what they really are.

In the light of Ephesians 1:7, you and I must be willing to confess and renounce all sin. We must be willing to forgive all other persons who have ever trespassed against us, or harmed us, or wronged us as we would have God forgive us. If we take that action, on that basis, we are then able to make the testimony that through the blood of Jesus, all our sins are forgiven.

SOLD UNDER SIN

You may remember that in the last chapter we looked at First Peter 1:18-19, which says:

> ...knowing that you were not redeemed with corruptible things, like silver or gold, from your aimless conduct received by tradition from your fathers, but with the precious blood of Christ, as of a lamb without blemish and without spot.

The blood of Jesus was the price of our redemption. We were in the devil's grip. We were his legitimate prey. But

Jesus bought us back at the price of His blood, the only price that could redeem a fallen human race.

In Romans 7:14, Paul says:

...I am carnal, sold under sin.

The metaphor Paul is using would be totally familiar to us if we were knowledgeable about the civilization of that day. Much of Roman and Greek civilization was based on slavery. There was a substantial substratum of slaves in both societies, and it was common for people to be sold as slaves in a slave market. A common Latin phrase of that day was *to sell a person under the spear*, which meant to sell him as a slave. In the slave market of those days, there was a pedestal on which they placed the person who was up for sale. Over his head there would be stretched a spear, which was the token that he was being sold as a slave.

When Paul says, "*I am carnal, sold under sin,*" what he is saying is, "My sin is the spear over my head that exposes me for sale in Satan's slave market." At one time in our lives, that is where every one of us was—waiting to be sold as slaves.

A SLAVE'S EMPLOYMENT

It is remarkable to think about a slave's employment. One woman is sold as a slave and becomes a cook. Another is sold and is used as a prostitute. It is not her choice. It is the choice of the slave owner. One man can be sold as a slave and become an agricultural worker. Another can be sold into slavery for employment in some vile practice. He has no choice.

That is why, though you and I may have been more "respectable" slaves, we must be careful not to look down on those less respectable. It wasn't their choice; it was the slave master's choice. We shouldn't despise the prostitute or the alcoholic. They were sold as slaves and they had no choice— it was the slave master who decided what their life would be.

When you and I were thus exposed for sale into slavery, Jesus walked into the slave market and said, "I'll buy that man. I'll buy that woman. What is the price? My blood." That is what it means to be redeemed by the blood of Jesus. If you can't get excited about that, you have never understood what Jesus has accomplished on your behalf by shedding His blood for you.

THE REALITY OF REDEMPTION

The truth of Jesus' redemption has never become a reality for most people. The only Person who can make the reality of redemption real to us is the Holy Spirit. Some people laugh at those who get excited to the point of jumping, shouting, and dancing. But when we know what God has done for us, we can hardly keep ourselves from jumping and dancing.

The Holy Spirit gives us the logical reaction to this good news. You and I were lost souls going to a lost eternity. Why wouldn't we exult about being freed by our Savior? God, for no reason but love, gave His perfect, spotless Son to die in our place. So, should we respond in a monotone voice, droning away as we say, "I believe in God the Father...." If we respond that way, do we really believe? Because if we did, our response would be different. A lifeless response is religion; when we have faith, it transforms us entirely.

Side by side with First Peter 1:18-19, I always like to place Psalm 107:2:

> *Let the redeemed of the Lord say so, whom He has redeemed from the hand of the enemy.*

Who is the enemy? Satan. What do we have to do if we are redeemed? We actually have to *say* that we are redeemed. It is part of our testimony.

THE ATOMIC AGE PSALM

Psalm 91 has been called "the atomic age psalm" and "the psalm of perfect protection from every kind of evil and danger and harm," however and whenever it may come. You may know this beautiful psalm very well, so I won't quote it in its entirety. Let's just turn our attention to the first two verses:

> *He who dwells in the secret place of the Most High shall abide under the shadow of the Almighty.*

The word *abide* in Hebrew normally means *to pass the night*. It is a word that is frequently used as a reference to "spending the night." So, during the hours of darkness, the true believer will be under the shadow or protection of the Almighty. Let's look now at the second verse:

> *I will say of the Lord, "He is my refuge and my fortress; my God, in Him will I trust."*

These phrases are the antechamber or entrance—the way into the complete protection of the remaining verses. What opens the door? It is *your* testimony: "*I* will say." If you don't say it, you don't have it. It takes some courage to say what follows in Psalm 91. But only those who *say* it have the scriptural right to live in it. It is the word of our testimony that makes it effective.

The reality comes through our testimony. So let's say it. My personal testimony is this:

> *Through the blood of Jesus, I have been redeemed out of the hand of Satan. Through the blood of Jesus, all my sins are forgiven.*

I was in the hand of Satan; I am no longer in his hand. I have been redeemed out of his hand. It was the blood of Jesus that got me out of the hand of the devil, the life-taker, and into the hand of the Good Shepherd, the Life-Giver. Further, Jesus said, "No man shall pluck them out of My hand." There was a transfer of my life from the devil's hand to the hand of the Lord.

By testifying to this wonderful truth, you are doing something of tremendous spiritual significance, which can affect the rest of your life. Your testimony is being witnessed by hosts in heaven. Your testimony is the hyssop that gets the blood to where you live.

Chapter 10

CLEANSING

THE SECOND APPLICATION OF THE BLOOD OF JESUS IS *cleansing*. In regard to cleansing, the first scripture we will consider is First John 1:7.

> *But if we walk in the light, as He [Jesus] is in the light, we have fellowship with one another, and the blood of Jesus Christ His Son cleanses us from all sin.*

In this verse, it is important to see that there are three verbs in the continuing present tense. To emphasize that point, we could paraphrase the verse as follows: "If we continue walking in the light, we continue having fellowship with one another, and the blood of Jesus continues to cleanse us." It is imperative to see that the use of the word "if" in this verse makes it clear that all the promised results are conditional. They depend upon obedience to the condition.

It is also important to notice, before we take the application of the blood in this passage, that there are three actions that are interrelated or bound together in the Word of God that cannot be separated. These three actions are walking in the light, fellowship with one another, and the cleansing of the blood.

CONDITIONAL CLEANSING

I have met scores of people who claim the cleansing and protection of the blood but who did not meet the conditions that entitle them to receive such cleansing and protection. Cleansing through the blood of Christ is a consequence that follows from something that is stated by an *if.* It is conditional upon our fulfilling the condition stated in the *if.*

If we walk in the light as He is in the light, then two results follow. Not one, but two. The cleansing of the blood is the second result. The first result is that we have fellowship with one another. The second result is that the blood of Jesus cleanses us from all sin.

Logically, if we are not in fellowship, it serves as proof that we are not walking in the light. Conversely, if we are not walking in the light, it follows that we cannot claim the cleansing of the blood of Jesus.

Ultimately, we come to this conclusion: if we are out of fellowship, we are out of the light. And if we are out of the light, the blood no longer cleanses us.

ONLY IN THE LIGHT

One of the most important principles I can offer at this point is this: the blood of Jesus cleanses *only* in the light. I have heard hundreds of Christians deceive themselves about their right of access to the blood. Although they keep quoting the latter part of First John 1:7, they never fulfill the condition stated in the *if*.

We *have* to walk in the light as He is in the light. The evidence we are walking in the light, first and foremost, is that we have fellowship with one another. Out of fellowship; out of the light. Out of the light; no longer under the cleansing of the blood. This is exactly the way it is. Fellowship is the place of light.

Fellowship is a place of testing. Why? Because the closer the fellowship, the brighter the light. Until you and I come to the place where there are no hidden corners, no shadows, nothing swept under the rug, and nothing covered up, we will not be out in the light. Such a transparent place is a very frightening place for the natural man. But that is the only place where the blood of Jesus fully fulfills its function of cleansing. If you want cleansing, it is in the light. If you are in any way wrong with God or wrong with your neighbor, you are not fully in the light. Consequently, the blood will never be applied except in the light.

What do you and I have to do? We have to come to the light. What does it mean to come to the light? We have to confess our sins and bring them to the light. That is one of the hardest steps for natural man to take. The light seems so bright. "Oh, I couldn't bring that terrible thing, that awful memory, that guilty secret, I couldn't expose it to the light."

The natural man shrinks from it. But the truth is that when it gets to the light, it disappears. Why? Because then the blood cleanses it. Sadly, if you don't bring it to the light, you keep it. This is a tremendously important principle—the blood operates *only* in the light.

COMPLETELY CLEANSED

When I lived in East Africa for five years, I was exposed to the Swahili language. I didn't exactly learn it fully, but I got involved in it enough to understand a little of it. In Swahili, there is a special tense that describes something which is complete and permanent. In that well-known song, "The Blood of Jesus Cleanses Us from All Sin," Swahili speakers say, *"Damu ya Yesu husafisha kabisa."*

The Swahili tongue also has some Arabic roots—an offshoot of the Arab traders who plied their wares up and down the east coast of Africa. So, if one knows Arabic, they will know that *"Damu ya Yesu"* refers to the blood of Jesus. *Husafisha* is "to cleanse." *Hu* means *it does it completely* or *totally.* *"Damu ya Yesu husafisha kabisa"* tells us then that the blood of Jesus cleanses us completely, totally, or absolutely from all sin. That translation has always stuck with me because it says it so perfectly.

When you and I meditate on the cleansing of the blood of Jesus, we need to think of something that is both continual and complete. This is how we can testify to this truth concerning the cleansing power of the blood of Jesus:

While I walk in the light, the blood of Jesus is cleansing me, now and continually, from all sin.

There is a beautiful commentary on this concept in Psalm 51, which is the great penitent psalm of David after he had been convicted of his sins of adultery and murder. I believe it to be one of the most beautiful psalms ever written. I think that every one of us does well to read it from time to time as our own prayer. (I believe in making the psalms my prayers. I don't just read them, I read them as my prayers.) In verse 7, David says:

Purge me with hyssop, and I shall be clean; wash me, and I shall be whiter than snow.

From our earlier chapters, we take note that David introduces the use of hyssop. What is the implication of the hyssop? It is the means by which I bring the blood to where I am. It is a prophetic preview of being cleansed with the blood of Jesus.

As you read this verse, I would encourage you to make it a prayer and not just say it as an exercise. Psalm 51:7: "Purge me with hyssop, and I shall be clean; wash me, and I shall be whiter than snow." Isn't that a beautiful thought?

With this verse in mind, let's repeat the testimony we just learned:

> *While I walk in the light, the blood of Jesus is cleansing me, now and continually, from all sin.*

I say in this declaration that the blood of Jesus is cleansing me now. Why do I say this? Because I always believe in a here-and-now statement. Not just something general, but real in the present moment. It is cleansing me here now. But it is also continual.

What an assurance it is to know where you and I can go when we are guilty! Stop for a moment and think about the billions of people who are guilty and do not know where to go. Imagine what it would be like to have a guilty conscience—to be tormented with the impact of your sin—and not know where to go to find forgiveness and peace. That is the condition of humanity today.

Chapter 11

JUSTIFICATION

THE NEXT EFFECT OF THE BLOOD OF JESUS IN OUR LIVES is *justification*. The word *justification* is a rather tiresome theological term that often obscures its true meaning. We will look first at the root of the word, and then I will explain how I understand justification.

THE RIGHTEOUSNESS CONNECTION

The real theme of the epistle of Romans—one that I find very exciting—is *righteousness*. Many centuries before Paul wrote the letter to the Romans, Job had asked the question: "How can a man be righteous before God?" (Job 9:2). The book of Romans is God's answer.

The central theme of Romans is righteousness—so if you are interested in righteousness you will be interested in Romans. To put it another way, if you aren't interested in Romans, it is rather likely you are not interested in righteousness.

In His Sermon on the Mount, Jesus said, "Blessed are those who hunger and thirst for *righteousness.*" Not blessings, not healings, and not prosperity. You can hunger and thirst after all those benefits without being blessed. But when you get hungry and thirsty for righteousness, *then* you get blessed. If you are hungry and thirsty for righteousness, at one time or another you have to come to grips with Romans.

We find a connection between righteousness and justification in Romans 5:8-9:

> *But God demonstrates His own love toward us, in that while we were still sinners, Christ died for us. Much more then, having now been justified by His blood, we shall be saved from wrath through Him.*

First, I want to point out to you that Jesus, in giving His life-blood for us, provides a demonstration and proof of

His great love for us. We discovered this truth in our study of the parables of the treasure in the field and the pearl of great price. Now this verse affirms as well that we have also been justified by His *blood*.

A CHANGE IN CHARACTER

In both Hebrew and Greek there is one word that is either translated *just* or *righteous*. In Hebrew, it is *tsaddiq* and in Greek it is *dikaiosune*. But whether the word is translated *just* or *righteous*, it is the same word. In English, it is more problematic. We have a subtle difference between *just* and *righteous*.

When considering the word *just*, we tend to think in terms of legality and law. With *righteousness*, we think in terms of character and conduct. But there is no such division in the language of the Bible. Our having been justified by His blood means we have been made righteous by His blood.

The word translated *justified* has a whole array of related meanings. First of all, it has a legal meaning. It means that when you are justified, you are acquitted. You are on trial, but you have been acquitted. That is good news! Think of what a person must feel when he is being tried for murder and finds out that he is acquitted. If you can imagine such a feeling—that is how you should feel about justification. It should make you that happy.

Second, you are not guilty.

Third, you are *reckoned* righteous. Many Christians stop there, but I assure you that the full meaning of the word is more than that. It is "you are *made* righteous." The blood of Jesus does not merely cause you to be reckoned righteous. It makes you righteous.

The word *justified* is also another way of saying "just-as-if-I'd" never sinned. This is because I have been made righteous with Christ's righteousness, which has no evil past and no shadow of guilt. Therefore, Satan can find nothing whatever to say against me. You and I need to recognize that we are not justified unless we have been *made* righteous. It is more than a legal ceremony. It is more than a change of labels. It is a change in our character and life produced by the blood of Jesus.

THE GIFT OF RIGHTEOUSNESS

In my teaching on *The Divine Exchange*, one of the statements that I derive from Scripture is the following: *Jesus was made sin with our sinfulness that we might be made righteous with His righteousness.* Being made righteous with His righteousness, you are justified. There is no guilt and there is no problem with the past. It has all been erased.

Romans 3:24-25 makes this point so very clear to us:

> *...being justified [made righteous] freely by His grace through the redemption that is in Christ Jesus...*

I am glad the word *freely* is present in that verse, because God gives it to us as a *gift.* One of the problems with religious people is that they are always trying to earn justification—and they never arrive. They are never satisfied or relaxed, because they think they have to do just a little bit more to be made righteous. It will never work. Let's repeat verse 24 and add on a little more:

> *...being justified freely by His grace through the redemption that is in Christ Jesus, whom God set forth as a propitiation by His blood, through faith...*

We are justified through faith in the blood of Jesus. As a further commentary on this point, we need to look briefly at Romans 4:4:

Now to him who works, the wages are not counted as grace but as debt.

The misconception for many Christians is expressed like this: "I have always lived right and always done my duty. God owes it to me. God *has* to give it to me; it is a debt." But in actual fact, God doesn't owe anything to anybody.

To confirm this, let's look at the beginning of verse 5:

But to him who does not work but believes...

What is the first step you have to take? Stop doing anything. Stop trying to make yourself righteous. Stop trying to be a little better. Call a halt to all that. What do you do? Just believe. Is it that simple? If it isn't that simple, you and I will never make it.

Please note the wonderful truth in verse 5:

But to him who does not work but believes on Him who justifies the ungodly, his faith is accounted for righteousness.

God makes unrighteous people righteous. That is what the Scriptures say, and I believe it!

We see a similar truth in Second Corinthians 5:21:

For He made Him who knew no sin to be sin for us, that we might become the righteousness of God in Him.

I like to put in a few names in places of the first few pronouns: "For God made Jesus, who knew no sin, to be sin for us, that we might be made the righteousness of God in Him."

This verse expresses the complete exchange that I quoted at the beginning of this section: Jesus was made sin with our sinfulness that we might be made righteous with His righteousness. This righteousness is available through faith in His blood. We are made righteous through faith in the blood.

HIS RIGHTEOUSNESS

An oft-quoted command of Jesus—Matthew 6:33—is so often misunderstood:

Seek first the kingdom of God and His righteousness [not your own].

It is said of the Jewish nation in Romans 10 that they, going about to establish their own righteousness, have not submitted themselves unto the righteousness which is of

God by faith in Jesus Christ. It takes humility to accept the righteousness of Jesus Christ. Why? Because it means, first of all, that you have renounced every shred of your old self-righteousness.

Many Christians are surprised by what Isaiah 64:6 says:

All our righteousnesses are like filthy rags.

Not all our *sins*, but all our *righteousnesses* are as filthy rags in the sight of God. As long as you and I flaunt the filthy rags of our church membership, our self-righteousness, our good deeds, our piety, the devil will tear us to shreds in the presence of God. But when you and I come to the place where we are relying on nothing and on no one but the Word of God, the blood of Jesus and the righteousness which is by faith in Christ, we are no more a target for the devil. There is nothing in us that he can put his finger on or bring up by way of accusation before God.

RESULTS OF RIGHTEOUSNESS

True righteousness should produce certain immediate and definite observable results in our lives. Let's take a few moments to examine some of them as stated in Scripture. Actually, the entirety of our way of living, our attitude, our relationship, and the effectiveness of our Christian life and service will depend on how much we realize that we have been made righteous. Proverbs 28:1 says:

> *The wicked flee when no one pursues, but the righteous are bold as a lion.*

We don't see very much boldness among most Christians today. Most are often timid and apologetic. They tend to back down when confronted with evil or the devil. The real root cause could well be that they have not appreciated the fact that they are righteous in God's sight—as righteous as Jesus Christ Himself. When you and I appreciate that, it makes us bold.

Isaiah beautifully states another result of righteousness:

> *I will greatly rejoice in the Lord, my soul shall be joyful in my God; for He has clothed me with the garments of salvation, He has covered me with the robe of righteousness* (Isaiah 61:10).

Isaiah is celebrating two provisions—*salvation* and *righteousness*. When you trust in Jesus Christ and His sacrifice on our behalf, we will be clothed with a garment of salvation. But it does not stop there—you and I will be *covered* with the robe of righteousness. One translation says He has "wrapped me [around] with the robe of righteousness" (NASB).

May I give you this encouraging word? You are totally covered with the righteousness of Jesus Christ. The devil has nothing he can say against you. If he reminds you of everything you have done wrong, agree with him. Say, "You're quite right, Satan. But that's all in the past. Now I am clothed with the righteousness of Jesus Christ. See if you can find anything wrong with that!"

Isaiah cites some more results of righteousness. Isaiah 32:17 says:

> *The work of righteousness will be peace, and the effect of righteousness, quietness and assurance forever.*

According to this verse, there are three products of righteousness—peace, quietness, and assurance. They all come from the realization that we have been made righteous with the righteousness of Jesus Christ. It brings us boldness, peace, quietness, and assurance.

Moving to a similar thought in the New Testament, Romans 14:17, a familiar Scripture, says:

For the kingdom of God is not eating and drinking, but righteousness and peace and joy in the Holy Spirit.

All these qualities are products of righteousness. If we don't receive the righteousness by faith, we will struggle and try for all these other qualities but not achieve them. It is pathetic to see Christians trying to be joyful, trying to have peace, trying to relax, or trying to be assured—all because somebody has told them they ought to be!

My experience is that when a believer truly walks in the assurance of sin's forgiveness and righteousness by faith, it just happens. Joy flows naturally. Peace isn't an effort. Assurance is there. Boldness expresses itself. When this doesn't occur, the root problem is that believers need to realize they have been made righteous with the righteousness of Jesus Christ—justified.

RELIGION VERSUS RIGHTEOUSNESS

Ironically a great majority of religious people actually think they are more holy if they go around pointing out how sinful they are. The general religious attitude is that a person would be very conceited if they claimed to be righteous. These same people will often say that you are very religious if you keep speaking about your failures, your inconsistencies, and how many mistakes you have made.

I was brought up in a church where we had to make those kinds of statements every Sunday morning. We had to say, "Pardon us, miserable offenders. We have erred and strayed from Thy ways like lost sheep; we have done those sins which we have not ought to have done, and we have left undone those things which we ought to have done. And there is no health in us."

I always felt a certain reluctance in saying those words. Somehow, I knew I didn't want to be classified as a miserable offender. When I looked at the other offenders, I certainly agreed that they *were* miserable. Eventually I said to myself, "If all religion can make me do is to be a miserable offender, I can be an offender without religion—and not half so miserable!" So that is exactly what I eventually became—a far less miserable offender.

I could not say those words now. I would be a hypocrite. First of all, I believe I have divine health in Jesus Christ. Second, how could I pray for victory over sin on Monday morning if I know that six days later, on Sunday morning, I will have to say that I have erred and strayed, I have done those things which I oughtn't have done and left undone those things I ought to have done?

Can you see the problem? Such statements completely undermine the basis of my faith. Yet it sounds so good. You may be horrified when you hear me say that, but I tell you that I mean every word of it. I have been through it and twenty years was enough!

Here is my testimony about justification through the blood of Jesus:

> *Through the blood of Jesus, I am justified, acquitted, not guilty, reckoned righteous, made righteous, just-as-if-I'd never sinned.*

That is my testimony that gets the blood to where I live. I would encourage you to say it more than once. The more I testify to this truth from God's Word, the better I feel. The result? Knowing I am righteous in Jesus gives me great boldness, quietness, assurance, peace, and joy.

Chapter 12

SANCTIFICATION

THE NEXT APPLICATION OF THE BLOOD OF JESUS THAT I
want to share with you is *sanctification*.

Sanctification is another one of those long words whose
meaning is sometimes obscured. In essence, *to sanctify* is
directly related in the original languages to the word for
holy. So, *to sanctify* is *to make holy*. The English word *sanctify* is related to the word *saint*. Thus, *to sanctify* is *to make
saintly* or *holy*.

THE COVENANT

In this first section, let's take two scriptures from the book
of Hebrews to demonstrate the sanctifying power of the
blood of Jesus. We will look first at Hebrews 10:29, which

speaks about a person who is an apostate. This is a person who turns back from the Christian faith, having known it at one time, but turning away from it with a deliberate denial and rejection of the Lord Jesus Christ. The passage goes on to mention all the sacred parts of the faith that he renounces and, in a sense, defiles.

> *Of how much worse punishment, do you suppose, will he be thought worthy who has trampled the Son of God underfoot, counted the blood of the covenant by which he was sanctified a common thing, and insulted the Spirit of grace?*

Please notice that the verse speaks about treading underfoot the blood of Jesus. This reference comes in relation to the Passover ceremony, where the blood was applied to the lintel and the door posts, but not to the threshold. We are *never* to show disrespect for the blood of Jesus. But here is a person who has been sanctified by the blood of the New Covenant then turns back away from it. The main point for our discussion here is not so much that people turn back from the faith, but the fact that we are sanctified by the blood of the covenant.

The second verse from Hebrews that we want to examine is in chapter 13, verse 12:

> *Therefore Jesus also, that He might sanctify the people with His own blood, suffered outside the gate.*

This refers to the fact that Jesus was crucified outside of the city as a sin offering, which could not be offered in the compound of God's people.

SET APART

In the matter of our sanctification or holiness, there are some important considerations. To be counted holy or set apart to God, I have to offer the right testimony. There are two aspects to this—what we are set apart *from*, and what we are set apart *to*. We are set apart from sin and from everything that defiles, and then we are made holy with God's own holiness.

To be sanctified is to be removed from the area of Satan's visitation and stationed in an area where you are available to God but not at home when the devil calls. The one who is sanctified is in a place spiritually where God has access to him but the devil does not. That is what it means to be sanctified—set apart to God, made holy.

Similar to the process of our righteousness, sanctification, or holiness, does not come by works, efforts, or by religion. It comes by faith in the blood of Jesus. "Jesus, that He might sanctify the people with His blood, suffered outside the gate." To be sanctified is to be set apart to God. Anything that is not of God has no right of approach to you and it is kept away by the blood.

A REDEMPTIVE DIFFERENCE

To be set apart in sanctification and holiness establishes a distinction in who we are. God told Pharaoh in Egypt that he would set a redemptive difference between the people of Egypt and the people of Israel. The plagues that came upon Egypt would not come upon Israel, even though they were also dwelling in Egypt. Why did this happen? Because there was a redemptive difference. The redemptive difference in our lives is the blood of Jesus. We are set apart to God by the blood of Jesus.

Did you know that it was never God's will that His judgment on the wicked would also come upon the righteous? I cannot take the time to go into this principle here, but it is a fact that all Scripture confirms. (See Genesis 18:25 for an example.) If I am set apart to God by the blood of Jesus, then God's judgments on the wicked should never fall on me. I am set apart. I am not in the spiritual territory where those judgments apply.

TOTALLY TRANSLATED

In this connection, let me provide just one verse from Colossians. It is Colossians 1:13-14, but I will begin with verse 12 for context. Speaking in the plural in the first person on behalf of all believers, Paul says:

> *Giving thanks to the Father who has qualified us to be partakers of the inheritance of the saints in the light. He has delivered us from the power of darkness and conveyed us into the kingdom of the Son of His love, in whom we have redemption through His blood, the forgiveness of sins.*

Please notice that darkness *does* have power. Satan has authority over the disobedient because of their disobedience.

Despite Satan's power, we have been removed, through faith in the blood of Jesus, from the area of Satan's authority. We have been conveyed or translated into the kingdom of God and of Jesus Christ. In the Greek, the word *convey* (*translate* in the KJV) means "to carry over from one place to another place." In the Scriptures, it is used of a *total* transfer.

In the Old Testament, there were two men who were translated from earth to heaven. Enoch and Elijah—both went entirely in bodily form to heaven. All that Elijah ever left behind was his mantle, but his body went to heaven. As I understand Scripture, this is the truth for us too—we have been totally translated. We aren't *going* to be; we have *already* been translated—spirit, soul, and body. We are *not* in the devil's territory or under the devil's laws. We are in the territory of the Son of God and under His laws.

TWO OPPOSING LAWS

Both the devil's law and God's law are stated in Romans 8. The devil's law is the law of sin and death. But the law of God's kingdom is the law of the Spirit of life in Christ Jesus. It would be good for us to study that verse for a moment, because it describes here the two kingdoms with their opposing systems of law in operation. In Romans 8:2, Paul is making his personal testimony:

*For the law of the Spirit of life in Christ Jesus
has made me free from the law of sin and death.*

I am *not* in the devil's territory and I am *not* under the devil's law. His kingdom doesn't apply to me, because I am in another kingdom. I have been translated/carried over—spirit, soul, and body—through the blood of Jesus. That translation comes through being sanctified (or set apart) to God by the blood of Jesus.

PASSPORT REQUIRED

I want to make a comparison between resurrection of the body and being translated from one kingdom to another kingdom. The resurrection of Jesus in His body is a pattern for our resurrection. In a different light, Paul says in Philippians 3 that "our citizenship is in heaven" (verse 20). That truth applies to anyone who has been born again and committed himself or herself to live for Jesus. We live on this earth, and we are citizens of a country here on earth—but our real citizenship is in heaven.

If you are a citizen of a nation, you have the privilege of carrying a passport from that country. It is a proof of your citizenship. We, too, have a passport that identifies us as citizens of heaven—*the blood of Jesus.*

> *For our citizenship is in heaven, from which we also eagerly wait for the Savior, the Lord Jesus Christ, who will transform our lowly body that it may be conformed to His glorious body, according to the working by which He is able even to subdue all things to Himself* (Philippians 3:20-21).

Please notice the mark of a true Christian—that you and I are eagerly waiting for the Savior. The New King James translation of the phrase "our lowly body" is not a literal translation. The literal translation is very vivid: "He will transform the body of our humiliation that it may be conformed to the body of His glory."

Every one of us is continually reminded by our bodies that we are in a state of humiliation because of sin. But Jesus is going to change this body of humiliation into the likeness of the body of His glory. That is an exciting prospect—something to look forward to.

PARTAKERS OF HIS HOLINESS

Connecting with the "chastisement" of being reminded that our bodies are in a state of humiliation, the book of Hebrews carries a similar thought. It says that our earthly fathers chastised us for a short period of our lives according to their best judgment. But God does the same in a different way for a different result:

> *For they indeed for a few days chastened us as seemed best to them, but He for our profit, that we may be partakers of His holiness* (Hebrews 12:10).

Please notice again that we bring nothing to the table. We are not made holy through our own efforts to be holy any more than we are made righteous through our own efforts to be righteous. We partake of His holiness through the blood of Jesus.

Here is a potential verbal declaration to express that thought:

> *Through the blood of Jesus, I am sanctified, separated from sin, set apart to God, made holy with God's holiness.*

BOUGHT WITH A PRICE

In reference to our discussion of our physical bodies, I want to take the discussion one step further. In relation to the body of the believer, I have learned that proclamation regarding our bodies is where the blood of Jesus really begins to take effect. The declaration I have given you above is the most powerful one I have yet to discover for dealing with Satan and evil spirits. I have learned it by experience, and I have seen how it works.

To develop this idea further, let's look first of all at what the Scripture says about the body of the believer in First Corinthians 6:19-20:

> *Or do you not know that your body is the temple of the Holy Spirit who is in you, whom you have from God, and you are not your own? For you were bought at a price; therefore glorify God in your body and in your spirit, which are God's.*

Please notice that "bought with a price" takes us back to the theme of redemption. We have been bought back out of the hand of the devil at what price? The blood of Jesus. How much of us was bought back? Just our spirit? No. Our spirit and our body both belong to God. Why? Because Jesus paid the total redemption price of His blood for our entire being—physical and spiritual.

NO TRESPASSES ALLOWED

Please remember that you have been bought by Jesus; you don't belong to yourself. If you believe you own yourself, then you have not been bought with the blood of Jesus. You cannot have it both ways. You cannot belong to yourself and to the Lord. The Lord wants you for Himself; He has paid the price for you—His precious blood.

The passage from First Corinthians says we are to "glorify God" both in our body and in our spirit because both belong to God. Both have been redeemed out of the hand of the devil by the blood of Jesus. Neither my spirit, nor my soul, nor my body are any longer under the dominion or control of Satan.

Let me say this very clearly—I do not yet have a resurrection body. I have a mortal body. But that mortal body with every fiber, every cell, and every tissue is God's property, not the devil's. If the devil comes on this territory, he is trespassing. If I understand correctly my rights in Jesus, I can put up a sign and say, "No trespassing. Get out!" How is that possible? Because legally my body does not belong to the devil. It belongs to Jesus.

A PERSONAL RESIDENCE

Jesus has a special purpose for my body—it is to be the place of personal residence of the third person of the Godhead, the Holy Spirit. That is why my body is sacred. It is the appointed dwelling place of the Holy Spirit. Scripture says clearly many times over, "God does not dwell in temples made with hands."

Neither the Baptist church, nor the Episcopal church, nor the Catholic church, nor the Presbyterian church, nor the synagogue, nor any other church is the temple where God will dwell. He dwells in a temple that was not made with hands; it was made by divine workmanship according to divine purpose. That temple in which He dwells is the body of the believer, redeemed by the blood of Jesus Christ.

In First Corinthians 6:13 Paul says:

> *Foods for the stomach and the stomach for foods, but God will destroy both it and them. Now the body is not for sexual immorality but for the Lord, and the Lord for the body.*

Our bodies are not for unclean, immoral purposes—neither for fornication nor gluttony.

This came home to me recently when I was reading in the book of Proverbs. What I read arrested me: "The righteous eats to the satisfying of his soul" (Prov. 13:25). For a believer not to overeat is a mark of righteousness. Why? Because my body is the Lord's temple. I am not to defile it either by gluttony, nor by drunkenness, nor by immorality, nor by any other misuse. The body is for the Lord, and the Lord is for the body.

TENANT'S RIGHTS

When I present my body to the Lord, then He has the rights for my body. You see, if I purchase a property, I become responsible for its maintenance. If I live in a rented property, the landlord is responsible to maintain it. If you and I just let Jesus have a temporary right over our bodies like a tenant, He doesn't accept responsibility for the maintenance. But if Jesus owns our bodies, He is responsible to maintain them. That is the relationship that He desires. The body is for the Lord, and the Lord is for the body. My body is a temple of the Holy Spirit.

As we close this part of the chapter, I want to lead us toward a testimony and declaration that have great effectiveness. In my own experience, this testimony has literally proved to be dynamic. Sometimes in a deliverance service, people will ask, "Brother Prince, how do I know if I'm really free?"

I respond to them in this way: "One thing to do is to start testifying about the blood of Jesus." This approach will not work unless the Holy Spirit is present. But, if the power of God is in a meeting and people begin to testify to the blood of Jesus, you will sense things stirring up inside you. Basically, anything that resists the blood is of the devil. I encourage people to go on testifying until there is nothing more inside you that resists the devil. When the reaction stops, you can be pretty well assured you are clear.

As we have confirmed throughout the teaching of this book, we overcome him by the blood of the Lamb and the word of our testimony. What I am about to give you is the testimony I have proved by experience. When you get down to testifying about your body, that's when the fireworks really start to happen. Some people's religion is so spiritual that it doesn't do anything for them here on earth. It just doesn't deliver any results in the here and now.

Personally, I feel good every time I make this proclamation. I feel better each time I say it than I felt the time before.

> *My body is the temple of the Holy Spirit, redeemed, cleansed, sanctified by the blood of Jesus. Therefore, the devil has no place in me, and no power over me. My body is for the Lord and the Lord is for my body.*

You may find yourself feeling a little fearful to make that proclamation. Perhaps you are thinking, "Well, if I say that, all hell is going to break loose!" If that happens, don't worry. It is just a sure sign you have hurt the devil. My advice would be to continue with your testimony. When the storm is cleared, you will find you are in firmer possession of your territory.

Chapter 13

LIFE

NOW WE COME TO THE NEXT APPLICATION OF JESUS' blood, which is *life*.

You will remember that according to Leviticus 17:11, the life of all flesh is in the blood. When Jesus poured out His *soul*, He poured out His *life*. It is the blood that makes atonement for the soul. This means that the life of God—the life of the Creator—comes to us through the blood of Jesus.

Our human minds have no way to calculate the potential of that statement because the Creator is infinitely greater than all that He has created. Even so, it would be wonderful if we could grasp the totality of the power that is in the blood of Jesus. Do you remember what we said earlier? There is more power in one drop of the blood of Jesus than there is in the entire kingdom of Satan—because in the blood of Jesus is the eternal, uncreated, measureless life of God Himself. God's life is one that existed before anything was ever created.

I WILL RAISE HIM UP

In regard to the power of God's life operating in us, let's begin this chapter by looking at John 6:53-54:

> *Then Jesus said to them, "Most assuredly..."*

At various times and in various places, Jesus says either *assuredly* or *most assuredly*. Other translations say *verily* or *verily, verily*. Some of Jesus' most emphatic statements are introduced with *verily, verily*, or *most assuredly*. What he says in this passage represents one of those times. It is a statement that carries the top level of priority.

> *...Most assuredly, I say to you, unless you eat the flesh of the Son of Man and drink His blood, you have no life in you. Whoever eats My flesh and drinks My blood, has eternal life, and I will raise him up at the last day.*

Please notice that phrase: "I will raise him up." We must bear in mind that our redemption is not complete until the resurrection of our body. It is *only* completed at the resurrection.

In Philippians 3:7-11, Paul said:

> *But what things were gain to me, these I have counted loss for Christ...that I may gain Christ and be found in Him...that I may know Him and the power of His resurrection, and the fellowship of His sufferings, being conformed to His death, if, by any means, I may attain to the resurrection from the dead.*

It is very important for each of us to see the significance of the resurrection of the body. Unfortunately, many Christians have been given the impression that our bodies are *not* very important. Simply put, that is not *God's* estimate. God says our bodies are *very* important. Our bodies are temples for the Holy Spirit. They are wonderfully and fearfully made. God promises that He is not going to leave our bodies in a state of decay. He is going to resurrect them with glory like that which Jesus experienced. Redemption in its fullest outworking and consummation comes in by the resurrection.

OUR EARNEST EXPECTATION

The point we have just made is very important. Even so, I find a lot of Christians simply do not grasp the importance of the resurrection. Paul thought differently than that, as evidenced by what he said in Romans 8:18-19:

> *For I consider that the sufferings of this present time are not worthy to be compared with the glory which shall be revealed in us [at the resurrection]. For the earnest expectation of the creation eagerly waits for the revealing of the sons of God.*

When will the sons of God be revealed? At the resurrection. Everything in creation is waiting for it. Creation is on the tiptoe of expectancy. The trees, the seas, the rivers, the mountains are all waiting. It is extraordinary and ironic that all of creation is so very excited—yet, much of the Church is not excited at all.

We read more about creation's situation in verse 20:

> *For the creation was subjected to futility, not willingly, but because of Him who subjected it in hope.*

You see, all of creation suffered because of man's sin. There were no thorns and no thistles before man sinned. Nothing ever died. Nothing was corrupted. The situation continues in verse 21:

> *Because the creation itself also will be delivered from the bondage of corruption into the glorious liberty of the children of God.*

Not only are *we* going to come into our glorious destiny, but the *creation* is going to come too. However, God has assigned His priority—that creation will not come in until *we* come in. Creation asks longingly, "Why are you people so slow? Why aren't you excited? Why aren't you doing what's necessary to bring the close of the age?" This is the theme of verse 22:

> *For we know that the whole creation groans and labors with birth pangs together until now.*

Amazingly, every time Paul says, "we know," the fact is that most contemporary Christians *don't* know. We should know that the whole creation is in labor pains. Waiting for what? Waiting for the revelation of the sons of God, the birth of a new age, and deliverance from corruption.

Paul goes on to make another statement in verse 23 that, again, is not true of many Christians:

> Not only they, but we also, who have the first-fruits of the Spirit, even we ourselves groan within ourselves [that's intercession], eagerly waiting for the adoption, the redemption of our body.

Did you see the closing phrase? Everything Paul is writing about there in Romans 8 has a connection with the redemption of the body, the resurrection. None of what he describes will take place until the resurrection.

THE TRUE DRINK

Returning now to John 6, the first scripture we explored in this chapter, we make an interesting discovery. Four times in this chapter Jesus says about the believer, "I will raise him up at the last day." It is part of salvation, but it is predicated on something spoken in John 6:54-56:

> Whoever eats My flesh and drinks My blood has eternal life...

Not *will* have, but *has*.

...and I will raise him up at the last day. For My flesh is food indeed [or true food], and My blood is drink indeed [or true drink]. He who eats My flesh and drinks My blood abides in Me, and I in him.

Again, we need to understand that these verbs are in the continuing present tense. "He who continually feeds on My flesh, and continually drinks My blood, continually abides in Me and I in him." It is very clear from this passage that the Lord attaches tremendous importance to feeding on His flesh and drinking His blood. I am not the final authority, but I really believe He is talking here about communion.

Many years ago, I lived for a while in an Arab town with Arab Christians. When they wanted to have the Lord's Supper, they said, "Let us drink the blood of Jesus." What does this tell us? Those Arab Christians had the right picture. Drinking the blood of Jesus is *communion*. Our entire attitude toward this may be one of aversion: "I don't like the thought of drinking blood." It took me a number of years to come to grips with this statement. Even so, to have eternal life, we have to drink His blood and feed on His flesh.

Once again, we remember the pivotal statement in Leviticus 17:11, which tells us that the life is in the blood. If you and I want life, we have to appropriate the blood. I am not saying that communion is the only way to appropriate the blood, because I have taught how we can appropriate it by our testimony. But to me personally, this principle of eating His flesh and drinking His blood has become very important.

Paul says of communion in First Corinthians 11:25, "This do, as *often* as you drink it, in remembrance of Me." But many churches would tend to say "as *seldom* as you do it." Thankfully, that is not true of many of the liturgical denominations. I appreciate that tremendously. Some of the most beautiful services I have ever attended have been liturgical communion services. They have held on to the importance of regular communion.

OUR APPROACH TO COMMUNION

For many years, Ruth and I have made it clear that we don't expect everybody else to become like us. When I share some of our habits and practices, it is not with any expectation that you ought to do the same. Please don't take what I share in that way. Even so, Ruth and I came to the conclusion some years ago that we didn't have communion nearly often enough.

So, as the priest of our home, I felt free to say that we would have communion every day. So now we take it in our early morning time with the Lord. We always close that time by taking the bread and the wine. I am not saying every Christian should do that, I am just saying I am thankful we do it. Both Ruth and I feel that something vital would drop out of our lives if we omitted that practice.

I like to do it in a very simple way, and I like to be very specific. "Lord, we're doing this in the remembrance of You; we're proclaiming Your death." I must say that it is so wonderful in a place like Jerusalem, where we live for half the year, to proclaim the Lord's death when most people don't even believe in Him. Then I say, "We receive this bread as Your flesh and this wine as Your blood." Again, I am not recommending this practice specifically. But I am suggesting that as Christians, we do not avail ourselves of the life that is in the blood nearly as much as we need to.

LIFTED OUT OF TIME

When Ruth and I have communion together, we take note of what Paul says: "We proclaim Your death until You come." We remember these two aspects—the Cross and the Coming. We never start a day without reminding ourselves of those vital truths.

Somebody has said about the communion service that it lifts you out of time. In the communion, you have no past but the Cross, no future but the Coming. You do it in remembrance of the Cross until He comes.

Sharing our way of taking communion is not intended to change your way of celebrating this sacrament. But it is intended to stimulate you to consider whether you are taking the opportunity to avail yourself of the life that is in the blood.

To make a personal application of this truth, let's make the following declaration together:

> *Lord Jesus, when I receive Your blood, in it I receive Your life, the life of God—divine, eternal, endless.*

Chapter 14

INTERCESSION

THE LAST TWO APPLICATIONS OF THE BLOOD THAT WE will examine are somewhat unique and surprising. Both of them will take us out of the realm of time and into the heavenly and eternal realms—which is where we want to end up anyway.

The first provision for application may surprise you. It is *intercession*. Our main passages of focus will be from Hebrews 12.

YOU *HAVE* COME

Before we examine the sections of Hebrews 12 that have to do with intercession, it is important that we begin at verse 22. This verse, "You have come" is spoken in the perfect tense. In other words, it does not say, "You are *going* to come" but "You *have* come." In the Spirit, the designated place is where you have *already* arrived. In your flesh you are sitting on earth, but in your spirit you are in a different realm.

> *But you have come to Mount Zion, and to the city of the living God, the heavenly Jerusalem, to an innumerable company of angels, to the general assembly and church of the firstborn, [that is the born again ones] who are registered in heaven, to God the Judge of all, to the spirits of just men made perfect [which I believe are the saints of the Old Testament], to Jesus the Mediator of the new covenant, and to the blood of sprinkling that speaks better things than that of Abel* (Hebrews 12:22-24).

In that passage, eight destinations are listed to which we *have* already come:

1. To Mount Zion;

2. To the heavenly Jerusalem (not the earthly Jerusalem), the city of the living God;

3. To an innumerable company of angels;

4. To the church of the firstborn who are registered in heaven;

5. To God, the Judge of all;

6. To the spirits of just men made perfect;

7. To Jesus, the mediator of the New Covenant;

8. To the blood of sprinkling that speaks better things than that of Abel.

IT SPEAKS BETTER THINGS

The last destination in the list is *the blood of sprinkling*, or the sprinkled blood of Jesus that speaks better for us than Abel's blood. Let's ask ourselves a question about Jesus' blood. Where was it sprinkled? I would suggest that the blood of sprinkling is the fulfillment of the picture of the high priest. In the days of the tabernacle, the high priest sprinkled the blood seven times on the way into the holy of holies, and then he sprinkled it on the mercy seat. I believe there is a mercy seat in heaven; I also believe the blood of Jesus is sprinkled on heaven's mercy seat. I further believe that His blood does precisely what the writer of Hebrews says: *it speaks on our behalf.*

It is very interesting to me that Jesus' blood is contrasted with the blood of Abel in three ways:

- Number one, Abel's blood was shed against his will; Jesus gave His blood willingly.

- Number two, Abel's blood was sprinkled on earth; Jesus' blood was sprinkled in heaven.

- Number three, Abel's blood called for vengeance; the blood of Jesus calls for mercy and forgiveness.

In Genesis 4:10, God said to Cain, "What have you done? The voice of your brother's blood cries out to Me from the ground." Just as strongly as the blood of Abel cries for vengeance, the blood of Jesus Christ pleads for forgiveness and mercy. What does this mean for us? It is very important for us to grasp the fact that we have intercession going on for us continually—day and night in the presence of God—through the blood of Jesus.

EVEN WHEN WE CAN'T PRAY

When I was in Kenya in the late l950s, I was in a car accident that nearly cost me my life. The accident happened through no fault of mine. A gasoline lorry had preceded us on the road, leaving a slick of oil that caused our car to skid over a 9-foot embankment at 55 miles an hour. I am convinced that the car turned a complete somersault in the air, and it ended right-side up on its wheels with the engine still running. Actually, we were able to drive the car away from the scene, which was amazing.

There were three persons in the car at the time: my first wife Lydia, who was beside me in the driver's seat; me, the driver; and our little African baby, Jesika, who was just under a year old. She was in a baby basket on the lower half of the back seat that had been made flat in this station wagon.

When I found myself in the car at the bottom of the embankment, I knew something terrible had happened. Your first instinct, invariably, is to open the door. So, as I opened the door, I wondered why the ground was much higher than usual. I later discovered that when the car came down after flipping over the embankment, my weight had pushed the driver's seat right down onto the floor of the car. From that hard landing, I broke three vertebrae in my spine, which I didn't discover for quite a while.

The most amazing miracle was that our little baby was thrown forward out of the baby basket and ended up on the gear lever—but didn't hurt herself at all. (It was a little station wagon with very little headroom.) Lydia had been thrown backward out of the seat beside me and ended up completely jammed into the baby basket. Her head was right against her knees. Apart from a few scratches, Lydia was unhurt. I was the only one who was seriously injured.

After I had been in the hospital for some time, I began to feel as if my spirit had been displaced. I don't know whether you can understand this or not, but it was as if my spirit wasn't there to pray. I lay in the hospital knowing I needed prayer, yet unable to pray for myself.

In that situation, I became aware of an encouraging reality. Even when I couldn't pray, the blood of Jesus was still speaking on my behalf. Day and night, unceasingly, whether we are weak or whether we are strong, it speaks. Whether we are right or whether we are wrong, the blood of Jesus always speaks on our behalf. Always, it calls for mercy and forgiveness.

To close this chapter on intercession, let's declare a testimony about the blood of Jesus speaking on our behalf. We will make this a very personal declaration:

Thank you, Lord, that even when I cannot pray, Your blood is pleading for me in heaven.

Chapter 15

CONFIDENT ACCESS

WE COME TO THE SEVENTH AND FINAL APPLICATION OF the blood of Jesus. This application is also found in the book of Hebrews—a passage that also pertains to access into the Holy of Holies.

A NEW AND LIVING WAY

In Hebrews 10:19-22, we read:

> *Therefore brethren, having boldness...*

The Greek word translated *boldness* means *freedom of speech*. I believe most modern translations use the word *confidence*. We have *total* confidence. We do not need to be ashamed; we do not need to be timid, but we do have to be extremely reverent. Through the blood of Jesus we have total confidence.

> *...having boldness to enter the Holiest by the blood of Jesus...*

Where was the blood sprinkled? On the mercy seat in the Holiest of All—the most sacred place in the universe.

> *...by a new and living way which He consecrated for us, through the veil, that is His flesh...*

This verse tells us that we have a blood-sprinkled way into the Holiest.

> *... and having a High Priest over the house of God; let us draw near [draw near to the Holiest of All, to the mercy seat] with a true heart in full assurance of faith, having our hearts sprinkled from an evil conscience and our bodies washed with pure water.*

Here are the four requirements of the true worshiper mentioned in verse 22:

1. A true heart;

2. Full assurance of faith;

3. Our hearts sprinkled from an evil conscience;

4. Our bodies washed with pure water.

The pure water, I believe, is the Word of God. (Actually, I also believe it has an application to water baptism, but that is beyond the scope of this teaching.) We have boldness to enter into the immediate presence of God, the most holy place in the universe, through the blood of Jesus. His blood is speaking on our behalf.

A HIGH PRIEST

We also have a High Priest over the house of God who represents us in the presence of God, and that is Jesus. His priesthood is talked about in Hebrews 6:19-20. Speaking of the hope we have in Christ, the writer says:

> *This hope we have as an anchor of the soul, both sure and steadfast, and which enters the Presence behind the veil [that is the second veil], where the forerunner has entered for us, even Jesus, having become High Priest forever, according to the order of Melchizedek.*

There in the Holiest of All, we have the sprinkled blood of Jesus that speaks on our behalf. We have a blood-sprinkled way in, and we have a High Priest after the order of Melchizedek, king and priest in the immediate presence of God. All of those benefits to us center around His precious blood.

ONE DIRECTION ONLY

I don't know whether access into the Holy of Holies excites you, but it excites me tremendously. My experience has been that most Christians don't have even a glimpse of the significance of the tabernacle or the later temple. Few, if any, know that these are a type of the heavenly tabernacle. Hebrews 9:24 adds to our perspective, citing the connection between the earthly and holy places:

> *For Christ has not entered the holy places made with hands, which are copies of the true, but into heaven itself, now to appear in the presence of God for us.*

If I can accomplish one goal with this chapter, I will have achieved my most important objective. What is that goal? To spark a longing in you to head in one direction only—into the Holiest of All. Why? Because that is where we encounter God.

A NEW AND LIVING WAY

Let's turn again to our starting point in Hebrews 10, where we have a statement about the New Covenant and the high priesthood of Jesus. Verse 19 says:

> *Therefore, brethren, having boldness to enter the Holiest by the blood of Jesus...*

Under the Mosaic covenant, the way into the Holiest was not yet made manifest. But under the New Covenant, we have boldness to enter into the holiest by the blood of Jesus.

> *...by a new and living way, which He consecrated for us, through the veil, that is, His flesh...*

The torn veil that opens the way into the Holiest of All is the torn flesh of Jesus on the Cross.

> *...and having a High Priest over the house of God [that is Jesus], let us draw near with a true heart in full assurance of faith, having our*

> *hearts sprinkled from an evil conscience and our*
> *bodies washed with pure water* (Heb. 10:21-22).

We draw near through our faith in Jesus Christ. Through His atoning sacrifice on the Cross. Through His high priestly ministry on our behalf now in the presence of God. Through these provisions for us, we have what was not made available to the Jewish people under the Old Covenant. We have boldness to enter into the Holiest of All, which is also known as the Holy of Holies. The way into the Holiest of All has now been opened up for you and me. This is what I hope to discuss in this chapter—the access that we have through the blood of Jesus.

SIMPLY GOD

Even the very design of the tabernacle as a type is an invitation for us to draw near. The tabernacle was laid out with the north on the right-hand side, which is where north always is in Scripture. The entrance is from the east.

The whole area is divided up into three areas. There are different ways to apply this. It applies to the nature of God; it applies to the nature of heaven and many other topics. We can also see these three areas as the nature of man—spirit, soul, and body. The Outer Court represents the body; the Holy Place, the soul; and the Holy of Holies, the spirit.

There is always a conflict with the natural man when it comes to entering into the tabernacle, because the further you go in, the more confined, in a sense, the space becomes for you. Your options become fewer, and at the finish you end up in a smallish box 10 cubits by 10 cubits by 10 cubits with only one item of furniture.

That is just like God, you see. The Lord wants you to want *Him* without wanting anything else. It is not God plus blessing, or God plus healing, or God plus revelation, but simply *God*.

That is what the tabernacle speaks about—those who long to meet with God. Not for the sake of getting something, but because God is God. There is no higher privilege than just getting to meet with God.

That is the way into the Holiest and that must be our sole motivation. Without that motivation you and I will never get there. When the motivation is present, then you and I have to meet the requirements. Meeting the requirements is exactly what we are studying here, with particular reference to the blood of Jesus, which grants us access into the Holy of Holies.

I believe that with the help of the Holy Spirit, you can develop an understanding of your destination, the Holiest of All, and a longing in your heart to get there.

ENTERING IN

As we come into the Holiest of All, there is only one piece of furniture. It is the ark, which typifies Christ. It was a rectangular box of acacia wood overlaid with pure gold. There is the box overlaid with pure gold, and then there is the mercy seat, which typifies God's forgiveness and reconciliation.

As we learned in Chapter 3, on the Day of Atonement, the blood was sprinkled on the mercy seat representing the offering that dealt with sin. Over the mercy seat were the two cherubim—one cherub at either end turned with their faces toward the center of the mercy seat, having their wings reach out and touch tip to tip over the center of the mercy seat. The cherubim, I believe, typify worship and fellowship. Face-to-face represents fellowship. The outstretched wings and the bowed bodies are worship.

In the same way, when we come into the place of fellowship with God, we come to the place of fellowship one with another and we look each other in the face. The mercy seat is where we come to face-to-face fellowship with God and with one another.

In that place there is face-to-face fellowship over the mercy seat and the blood that was sprinkled there. That is the only place of true fellowship; it is in the spirit, it is face-to-face, it is over the mercy seat, and over the blood of Jesus.

May God bless you and may God help both you and me to meditate on this, because I have just touched the fringe of this whole area of truth. My desire is not to tell you everything but to get you to start searching for yourself.

HONORING THE BLOOD

As we have said continually in this book, it is so important to honor the shed blood of Jesus Christ. If the blood of Jesus were to be taken away, we would have no redemption, no cleansing, no justification, no sanctification, no life, no intercession, and no access. Everything hinges around the blood of Jesus. Let us never belittle or underestimate the blood.

I will say again what I said in an earlier chapter. If you want to know the difference between the soulish and the spiritual, any person who professes faith in Christ and does not honor the blood is *soulish*. The soulish man doesn't believe in the blood. In fact, it offends him.

This can be a diagnostic in our own lives as well. The soulish nature just doesn't like that statement, "Unless you eat My flesh and drink My blood you have no life in you." But it is the truth.

With thoughts of honor and reverence for the blood of Jesus, let's make a confession for the final statement:

> *Through the blood of Jesus sprinkled in heaven, I have access with confidence into the presence of God, into the Holy of Holies.*

I don't know whether our minds can truly grasp what we are saying when we make that declaration. But it speaks of our ultimate destination, the Holy of Holies in heaven, which is the most sacred place in the universe.

Chapter 16

CONCLUSION

As we come to the end of this book, I would like to put together the declarations about the blood of Jesus to which we have testified, making them into one proclamation:

> *We overcome Satan when we testify personally to what the Word says the blood does for us.*
>
> *Through the blood of Jesus, I have been redeemed out of the hand of Satan. Through the blood of Jesus, all my sins are forgiven.*
>
> *While I walk in the light, the blood of Jesus is cleansing me, now and continually, from all sin.*

Through the blood of Jesus, I am justified, acquitted, not guilty, reckoned righteous, made righteous, just-as-if-I'd never sinned.

My body is the temple of the Holy Spirit, redeemed, cleansed, sanctified by the blood of Jesus. Therefore, the devil has no place in me, and no power over me. My body is for the Lord and the Lord is for my body.

Lord Jesus, when I receive Your blood, in it I receive Your life, the life of God—divine, eternal, endless.

Thank You, Lord, that even when I cannot pray, Your blood is pleading for me in heaven.

Through the blood of Jesus sprinkled in heaven, I have access with confidence into the presence of God, into the Holy of Holies.

I would recommend that sometime during a time of prayer, you should go through this list and make your own personal confession for each testimony. Hopefully, as you take time each day in prayer, this list will be a help and a guide for you to make the right confession in the presence of the Lord. By making these proclamations, you will apply the blood to your life. You will do well to make this a habit, and it will help you learn to apply the blood in every situation.

HOLD FAST

Only *Jesus* is the Life-Giver. He shows His measureless love for us by the great price He paid to buy us back from the devil—His life-blood. Redemption, cleansing, justification, sanctification, life, intercession, and access. The blood of Jesus—sprinkled seven times—works in us in seven different ways. But remember, you overcome Satan by the blood of the Lamb and by the word of your testimony. That is how you enact His victory in your own life. That is how you apply the blood of the Lamb. Your persistence in this regard is what frightens the devil—and it is what will give you ongoing victory.

I can well remember when I first began to make this kind of testimony. I thought, "Well, I wonder where the devil will hit me next?" I know some people who won't testify, because they are afraid of what will happen when they do. But friend, that is just playing the devil's game. That is his way of keeping you from taking the action that is going to put you outside of his reach. It is *only* by the word of your testimony that you get the benefits of the blood.

You make your testimony once, and all hell breaks loose. All right. Praise the Lord! Say it again. The Bible says to "hold fast our confession" (Heb. 4:14). Then, when all hell breaks loose, the Word says, "let us hold fast the confession of our hope without wavering" (Heb. 10:23). So, we keep on saying it. It doesn't depend on your feelings. It doesn't depend on situations or symptoms or circumstances. Your testimony is as true as the Word of God. It is eternally true. Forever God's Word is settled in heaven.

THREE ETERNAL, UNCHANGING FORCES

I want to point out in closing that there is a relationship between the testimony of the Word to the blood and the operation of the Holy Spirit. You cannot leave the Holy Spirit out. Even more, by testifying to the blood, you bring the Holy Spirit into operation.

In First John 5:6, John is speaking about Jesus and he says:

> *This is He who came by water and blood—Jesus Christ; not only by water, but by water and*

blood. And it is the Spirit who bears witness, because the Spirit is truth.

I do not have time to go into this in any detail, but as I understand it, the water mentioned here means the Word of God. Jesus came as the *Great Teacher* teaching the Word, sanctifying and cleansing us by the washing of water by the Word. He came as the *Great Redeemer*, shedding His blood as the redemptive price. These are the two main aspects of His redemptive ministry—redeeming by the blood, and the sanctifying and cleansing by the washing of water by the Word. He did not come by the Word only. That is to say, He did not come as a Teacher only. But He also came as the redemptive Savior to give His life a ransom for many. This role as Savior in no way sets aside His other ministry as the Teacher.

Ephesians 5:26-27 testifies to this dual ministry of Jesus in the context of the Church:

> *That He might sanctify and cleanse her with the washing of water by the word, that He might present her to Himself a glorious church, not having spot or wrinkle or any such thing, but that she should be holy and without blemish.*

Here we have the double ministry of Jesus—by the water of the Word and by the shed blood of redemption.

HOLY SPIRIT HELP

When we bring the Word and the blood together, then it says the Spirit of God bears testimony because the Spirit is truth. As you and I begin to use the Word, stating what the Word says the blood does, the Spirit comes to us and bears testimony to the truth. All our best words can just be nice religious language. All of it may be very good language, and it may be doctrinally correct. But it doesn't do anything *until* the *Holy Spirit* bears testimony. But when the Holy Spirit bears testimony, then it becomes irresistible.

Do you remember my comment in Chapter 12? I made this statement: "None of this will work unless the Holy Spirit is present." I hope you can realize that there are no little rules and regulations in the Christian life—that if you do this, automatically it works. *Nothing* works without the Holy Spirit. But you can bring the Holy Spirit to work by testifying to the water of the Word and the blood, because *then* the Spirit bears witness. Then you have three eternal, unchanging forces at work on your behalf—the Word, the blood, and the Spirit.

Ecclesiastes 4:12 has tremendous application here:

...a threefold cord is not quickly broken.

When you begin to testify to what the Word says the blood does, the Spirit comes beside you to bear witness. Then you have the threefold cord—the Word, the blood, and the Holy Spirit.

What remains is for us to give thanks and praise to Jesus for all that He has done for us through His precious blood. Let's do just that to close out the teaching in this book.

Dear Lord Jesus,

I give You all the thanks and praise. You were willing to pour out Your life-blood to enable us to receive all that we have discussed in this book. We bless You and praise You for all You have done for us through Your precious blood. Amen.

ABOUT DEREK PRINCE

Derek Prince (1915–2003) founded Derek Prince Ministries International and authored more than a hundred books during his lifetime. He studied at Eton College, Cambridge University, and at the Hebrew University in Jerusalem. His daily radio broadcast, *Derek Prince Legacy Radio*, still reaches listeners around the world.

OTHER BOOKS BY DEREK PRINCE

They Shall Expel Demons

Pulling Down Strongholds

Secrets of a Prayer Warrior

Prayers & Proclamations

Rules of Engagement

Entering the Presence of God

Lucifer Exposed

The Gifts of the Spirit

Called to Conquer

Fasting

The Holy Spirit in You

Spiritual Warfare for the End Times

Bought with Blood